Praise for Andy Hilliard and *Synergea*

"Comprehensive. Concise. Clever. *Synergea* is the only book you need to create innovative and effective software."
—*Todd Ruback, Managing Director, FTI Consulting*

"Software development outsourcing requires a commitment to collaboration and cultural understanding. These two things create better businesses—and better businesspeople. Andy Hilliard spells it all out in *Synergea*, essential reading for today's software development leaders."
—*Jim Marascio, Principal & Chief Executive Officer, Equals 11*

"Building great software with multinational teams has become the key differentiator in successful organizations. In *Synergea*, Andy unlocks the secrets of creating great teams that span the globe."
—*Scott Prugh, CTO & Transformational Technology Leader*

"Andy Hilliard is the most passionate and experienced advocate for global software development I know. He knows that the best solutions come from building collaborative relationships among talented developers worldwide."
—*Paul Witkay, Founder & CEO, Alliance of Chief Executives*

"*Synergea* is a must-read for anyone looking to tap into the benefits of outsourcing and develop groundbreaking, efficient software. Andy's deep insights and perspective offer readers a unique and invaluable viewpoint on the subject."
—*Nacho De Marco, CEO at BairesDev & General Partner at BDev Ventures*

"While lower costs, faster time to market, and greater flexibility are obvious benefits of software development outsourcing, one of the best kept secrets about it is the rich rewards you get by working with people from different cultures. Being able to manage multinational teams will help any executive experience tremendous personal and professional growth. *Synergea* shows you how to do it right."
—*Andy Scott, Executive Coach for CEOs and Teams of High-Growth Companies*

"I cannot recommend this book highly enough. Andy Hilliard has provided today's executives and technologists with a masterclass in expanding talent networks for sustainable growth. It will quickly become the modern playbook for software outsourcing and should be required reading for anyone involved in strategic technology initiatives."
—David Beazley, Managing Partner, Alumni Ventures

"You won't find a more passionate proponent of software development outsourcing than Andy Hilliard. The information he shares in this smart guide covers secrets to multinational management you won't find anywhere else."
—Chris Coughlan, Founder & Principal, C Infinity Solutions

"*Synergea* encapsulates the essence of modern technology leadership. It equips readers with a blueprint for harnessing the power of collaboration through tech value networks, enabling them to create dynamic, highly effective software development teams. I wholeheartedly recommend this book to both seasoned leaders and aspiring technology visionaries seeking to stay ahead of the curve in an ever-evolving landscape."
—Andrew L. Bourne, CTO and Founder, CriticalGoals

"*Synergea* masterfully illustrates the necessity of tapping into global IT resources. As tech diversity grows, what Andy terms as 'multinational management' becomes vital for ensuring business agility and resilience. This isn't just about offshoring routine maintenance anymore; top-notch global talent is now accessible for the most advanced development tasks. *Synergea* offers invaluable insights on partnering internationally and ensuring cross-border readiness. It's essential reading for those struggling to source local IT talent or those facing agility issues due to IT resource limitations."
—Carole Kaufman, CTO, Impulse Logic, Inc.

"Andy provides key, up-to-date insights into the issues that leaders at modern software development firms struggle with in today's world. The real-world experiences in this book, from Andy and other experts in the field, will help anyone trying to build software products with teams from different countries and in different time zones."
—Mike Frey, Technical Executive Management

"*Synergea* captures Andy's wisdom for achieving global cooperation in software development, which is now table stakes for most firms—even 'non-software' companies. *Synergea* is effective as both a primer for those new to outsourcing, and a whetstone to sharpen the skills of those of us with decades of experience. Andy's insights on the human side of multinational management are particularly poignant, with practical insights, how-to frameworks, and concise case studies demonstrating his methods in practice."
—John Miniati, Coauthor of Kellogg's MBA Course, Product Management for Technology Companies

"As someone deeply entrenched in the world of software development outsourcing, I find *Synergea* to be a treasure trove of wisdom and practical advice. Andy Hilliard's approach to multicultural team management is both innovative and effective, making this book a vital tool for industry professionals."
—Michael Marmor, Consulting CTO and Venture Partner

"*Synergea* is an essential guide for leaders seeking to leverage global talent and build resilient, forward-thinking organizations in the digital age—I wish I had it when I was a tech CEO! Andy Hilliard skillfully navigates complexities such as remote teams, talent management, and AI integration, transforming these challenges into opportunities for innovation and efficiency."
—Adam Birnbaum, Executive Coach at ClearPath Group, Former CEO of PE-Backed SaaS Company

"There are huge benefits to tapping into a global workforce, but there are also plenty of traps for the unwary. Andy Hilliard does an amazing job of providing an overview of the opportunities and risks, so you can successfully leverage a world full of talent for your projects."
—Peter Bell, Founder/CTO, Geeks Who Lead & CTO Coach

"While *Synergea* is explicitly for CTOs and CPOs, it's also for non-technical leaders who want to up their talent game and team performance in a volatile marketplace. You'll glean a lot of great nuggets from Andy Hilliard's latest book!"
—Gary Frey, Author of Silence the Imposter: 7 Weapons to Silence Imposter Syndrome

"Knowing how to manage collaborative, geographically dispersed teams is the ticket to breakthrough ideas, high performance, and job satisfaction. *Synergea* gives software leaders a clear and inspiring blueprint to turbocharge their careers and gain job security for life."
—Dr. Heidi K. Gardner, Coauthor of Smarter Collaboration: A New Approach to Breaking Down Barriers and Transforming Work

"A revelation for tech leaders! *Synergea* underscores the critical importance of establishing a multinational development presence and an Agile operating model to drive superior business outcomes—faster, more cost-effectively, and with heightened competitiveness in our dynamic business landscape. Andy Hilliard offers invaluable strategies and practical advice for navigating the complexities of digital transformations."
—Roopa Sudheendra, Chief Product & Technology Officer

SYNERGEA

Also by Andy Hilliard

Outsource or Else!
How a VP of Software Saved His Company
(with Steve Mezak)

SYNERGEA

A Blueprint for Building Effective, Globally Distributed Teams in the New Era of Software Development

Andy Hilliard

ACCELERANCE
Redwood City, CA

Synergea: A Blueprint for Building Effective, Globally Distributed Teams in the New Era of Software Development

Published by Accelerance, Inc., Redwood City, California

ISBN 979-8-9898654-1-3 (paperback)
ISBN 979-8-9898654-0-6 (eBook)
Library of Congress Control Number: 2024900821

Address inquiries to: marketing@accelerance.com

For bulk discounts, or to book Andy Hilliard for a speaking engagement, contact marketing@accelerance.com.

Cover and interior design by Carolyn Jeffords

Copy editing by Ed Sweet

Manufactured in the United States of America

*To the Peace Corps and all its volunteers,
who commit years of their lives to build
relationships, exchange cultures and knowledge,
and transform communities for generations.*

CONTENTS

ACKNOWLEDGMENTS

It's always great fun to write a book, but just like software development it's not something I could ever do alone.

In fact, the idea for this book was brought to me by Lisa Morrell, who was working for Accelerance as CMO at the time. To be honest I didn't gravitate to the idea at first, but the more she pushed forward and talked about the possibilities the more excited I got. I'm deeply grateful to her for not giving up and having the patience for me to come around.

Other people on my team here at Accelerance helped shepherd the book from concept to completion. Rich Wanden, our Chief Customer Success Officer, became the day-to-day point person and made sure the project stayed on track on an aggressive timeframe. After we locked the manuscript, Rich passed the baton to Gunjan Jain, our Director of Strategic Initiatives, who capably moved the project forward into production and beyond.

Tom Cooper, a performance and productivity coach who leads many of our alignment workshops and runs his own consulting firm called the BrightHill Group, advised us on content and helped shape several of the chapters.

And Carolyn Jeffords, a talented graphic designer who's been working with our team since 2022, brought the book to life with an incredible cover and an engaging interior.

I'm extremely grateful to Leslie Willcocks, a professor at the London School of Economics, for contributing the Foreword. His ongoing research into IT outsourcing and digital transformation projects, backed by a storied history as a practitioner and advisor in the early days of software development, continues to shape and advance the industry. It's an honor to have his endorsement and a privilege to have gotten to know him and his work.

I also want to thank the 10 thought leaders who shared their unique and fascinating perspectives with me for the Guest Expert Spotlight sections at the end of each chapter. My discussions with Troy Hiltbrand, Guillermo Kopp, Ron Lichty, Patrick Mee, Rich Mironov, Pete Panagakis, Olivier Poulard, Erik Severinghaus, Jeff Shupack, and Rich Wanden added anecdotal and actionable insights to concepts and practices.

Ed Sweet, a Phoenix-based writer, helped me organize my thoughts and combed through vast amounts of source material that Accelerance has produced over the past few years. He was backed up by another Phoenician, Christine Leninger, whose editing skills tightened up the content and made each chapter even more readable.

And finally, I'd like to thank my wife Silvia—not only for giving me extra space and time to work on this project, but also for keeping my passion for Costa Rica and its rich and vibrant culture alive since we first met in 1990.

FOREWORD

Someone once said that an expert in any field is a person who knows enough about what's really going on to be scared. I would guess that Andy Hilliard and his colleagues have been scared many, many times. But, fortunately for you, the reader, they've been scared and scarred enough throughout their software development outsourcing journey so you don't have to be.

Synergea is a highly informative, engaging read. It is, above all, a very useful book. It only took me one sitting to get from cover to cover, and even though I'm highly experienced as a practitioner, researcher, and advisor in the fields covered I learned a great deal from Andy's explanations and guidelines on ways forward.

Andy probably asked me to contribute because I was in at the beginning of software development and IT projects in 1979 and have been tracking IT outsourcing and digital transformation since the early 1990s.[1] I sense that he saw me adding my own take on the content and not just providing an endorsement, however warranted. If so, here goes.

The book you hold in your hands is pervaded by an insight that continues to be learned the hard way: In any software development or

[1] See Willcocks, L., Oshri, I., and Kotlarsky, J. (eds.) (2023). *Transformation In Global Outsourcing: Towards Digital Sourcing of IT and Business Services*. Palgrave Macmillan, London and Willcocks, L., Hindle, J., Stanton, M., and Smith, J. (2023) *Maximizing Value with Automation and Digital Transformation: A Realist's Guide*. Palgrave MacMillan, London.

digitally-enabled business project, 75–85% of the challenges are generated by management, organisation, and people. Technology is responsible for a mere 15–25% of the challenges yet receives all the attention when problems arise. Developers are blamed as business leaders search for technical fixes to problems with no technical cause. Yes, you can technologize a poor process but all you will get is disaster faster.

Another insight I gained throughout my career involves the importance of knowing who owns a project. Early on, in what the Americans called the "Wild West" days of software development (in Britain the practice was referred to more euphemistically as a "craft"), we constantly ran into the same question: Is this an IT or a business project?

This seems amazingly naïve today, but the answer is foundational. It's all very well to treat a technology initiative as a specialist area when the system is self-contained within the IT function or deep in a back office somewhere, such as an internal accounting system. But when an IT project impacts front office processes or promises some unique business innovation, the specialist focus becomes much less useful.

Achieving significant business benefits in the latter scenario requires cross-functional collaboration among users, business managers, technical experts, and external resources—under committed, C-level leadership. This is far different from a project that merely requires the expertise of individual specialists governed by a detailed service contract and supervised by experts in IT.

The maturity of the technology also matters. If a technology is stable, has been used in the organisation before, and developers have the requisite skills, then it's fine for IT to own it. But with new and untested technologies, a business/user focus is preferable.

If you follow the logic, you can see how technological advances keep pushing software development and digital transformation projects further into the broader business realm. This poses a challenge for companies that need to stay competitive in the digital economy: Outsourcing is far more suitable for stable technologies and commodity (lower risk) activities, but it's becoming increasingly necessary to get innovative projects with far more complexity off the ground. Because of that, most companies need a lot of help strengthening collaboration processes on a global scale.

As the need for partnering ecosystems and multinational management have become table stakes for optimising software development, businesses like Andy Hilliard's Accelerance have become vital to the global sourcing marketplace: Synergea indeed!

From Agile to Agility

The 1980s saw the growth of structured methodologies for dealing with increasingly complex and resource-strained software development efforts. Projects were scaling bigger, talent was often in short supply, and knowledge needed to be embedded in repeatable management actions and better ways of organising.

By the 1990s, emerging technologies and dynamic global business contexts were forcing managers to think much more about adaptiveness and agility. I well remember a presentation by a Ford Europe executive in 1995, where he announced a "time box philosophy" for all projects going forward.

I had seen this used experimentally in software development activities before, but not as radically: Ford stipulated that every project must be completed within 90 days or less, focusing on core functionality at the expense of bells and whistles. Iterative prototyping with heavy involvement from users, business stakeholders, and external suppliers was the key operating mode, with the guiding principle that "80% systems are OK."

If a project could not be done in 90 days or less, it would not start. Larger projects could be broken down into digestible chunks, but delivery had to proceed along a planned trajectory "resulting in a town rather than a series of Portakabins," as the executive put it. To push the metaphors even further, my colleague at Templeton College, David Feeny, mused "Ahh, dolphins, not whales" when comparing small-scale projects that produce fast business value with large-scale, complex, and slow-moving projects with far-off end dates and deliverables. It's a phrase about projects that has stuck with me to this day.

After 1995, Agile methodologies for IT and business development programs became increasingly popular and the time box became increasingly smaller. The methodology has proven to be incredibly powerful, as long as people understand that working fast doesn't mean rushing to deliver something that jeopardises quality and performance.

These days, people are moving beyond Agile in search of true business agility. This need arises out of very dynamic business and global contexts, such as increased interconnectedness, complexity, and risk. The best way to lubricate business agility on the global stage is to understand the value of global teams and invest in their performance through effective management.

The best way to lubricate business agility on the global stage is to understand the value of global teams and invest in their performance.

The Evolution of Outsourcing

Andy Hilliard is rightly sceptical as to whether what he is doing can be called outsourcing. Using a strict academic definition, outsourcing is the handing over of activities, assets, and/or people to third-party management for required result. Over many years, professors Mary Lacity, Sara Cullen, and I found that IT and business process outsourcing works most effectively for well understood, stable, commodity type activities on three-to-five-year contracts, following a horses-for-courses, multi-vendor approach. This is the specialist focus I talked about above.

Relying on third parties is inherently risky, however, so a key question becomes "How do you mitigate the risks, especially when you're working on projects that push outsourcing outside of its comfort zone?"

As Andy writes, "Multi-partner, multinational management is fast becoming the new norm, as businesses work to future-proof operations through the creation of worldwide tech value networks, whose members can be called upon to provide the right skills at the right time. It's getting to the point where organisations that don't embrace multinational management models will be left in the dust."

Companies that employ good management practices—whilst retaining control over their digital and business destinies—can find great success with outsourcing. Back as far as 1998 we identified nine key capabilities for eliciting business requirements, leveraging external services, coordinating activities, and establishing and supporting a technology-process blueprint.

These nine roles require a small number of high performers and a distinctive mix of business, interpersonal, and technical skills. Interestingly, we found that many organisations downgraded their technical skills when in fact they needed them to have informed dialogue with external partners, deal with problems, and keep control over their IT destinies.

Towards Collaborative Innovation

Outsourcing has never been a great vehicle for technical, let alone business, innovation. But now that it's becoming mandatory for such activities, management and organisational models must transform accordingly.

As Andy and his team at Accelerance understand, this means more team working and additional client and supplier capabilities. Studying organisations that achieved collaborative innovation whilst working with external partners, we found nine keys to high performance, all of which are consistent with what you'll read as you get further into this book:[2]

Launching the relationship

1. Assign a great client/supplier leadership pair
2. Focus on business and strategic benefits over cost

[2] Lacity, M. and Willcocks, L. (2015). Nine Keys To World Class Business Process Outsourcing. Bloomsbury, London.

3. Drive strong transition, transformation, and change management capabilities

Keeping the relationship on target

4. Adopt a partnering approach to governance
5. Align the retained organisation, outsourced processes, and provider staff
6. Resolve issues together and fairly

Exploring new frontiers

7. Use technology as a performance enabler and accelerator
8. Deploy domain expertise and analytics
9. Prioritise and facilitate innovation

Simplicity Is Complex

To survive competitively, Ashby's Law of Requisite Variety states that the degree of environmental complexity an organisation faces must be matched by a corresponding degree of internal complexity—or variety—in its ability to model, create options, and take actions that can regulate the impacts of environmental factors and events.

In our studies of automation and digital transformation in organisations with major legacy issues—structure, processes, skills, technology, systems, and data—the hidden but serious problem is an imbalance between variety and simplification.

Albert Einstein highlighted the problem when he said, "Make everything as simple as possible, but no simpler." An experienced software development practitioner I know echoed the sentiment when he said, "There are two ways of constructing a software design: One way is to make it so simple that there are obviously no deficiencies, and the other way is to make it so complicated that there are no obvious deficiencies. The first method is far more difficult."

Simplicity has always been a difficult but very desirable goal in software development, and throughout this book Andy offers ways of controlling complexity rather than creating it. With these observations in mind, let me engage a little more thoroughly with the book's content and messages, including the fantastic Guest Expert Spotlights that appear at the end of each chapter.

Chapter 1 of *Synergea* evokes what I have come to call the new abnormal that characterises contemporary business environments. Andy is clearly correct about the need for a "quick pivot" management model that distributes risk and expands talent pools globally. My own work suggests that digitalized, flexible organisations will utilise core and peripheral workers in ways that offer functional, numerical, and financial flexibility.

Digital technologies offer three more flexibilities: locational (think remote working), temporal (think 24×7), and labour replacement/enhancement (through automation and online robo-sourcing). So far so impressive, but as Andy is very aware there are real management, organisational, and people challenges in operating such a model.

For example, how do you retain and develop the core workforce? Will the organisational culture erode from one based on commitment into a transactional one? How do you motivate peripheral workers of different types and skill levels? I like the ways forward Jeff Shupack suggests in Chapter 1's Guest Expert Spotlight—reduce functional silos, give people intent, and get out of the way.

Chapter 2 focuses on the use of virtual teams and hybrid work, while Chapter 3 deals with expanding the talent pool on a global scale. Andy spells out the need and the opportunity when he writes, "Skills access is a strategic imperative…Today, you can hire quality remote technology talent from more than 40 countries, which collectively represent about 40% of the world's population."

Patrick Mee gives many pieces of wisdom on working with distributed teams in Chapter 2's Guest Expert Spotlight, not least of which is to "give freedom and inspect frequently."

Pete Panagakis, the Guest Expert featured in Chapter 3, also offers advice that gels with our own findings: "I've found that it's always best to have as many senior and mid-senior people on your outsourced team as possible," he writes.

"You can add junior people later, but you're more likely to hit the ground running and achieve quick wins with people who have experience."

Moving on, Chapter 4 rightly deals with what makes people like Andy scared—the risks of unpreparedness. Many of these risks sound familiar: undefined metrics, inconsistent priorities, lack of executive champions, lack of team engagement, and poor partnership relations on the business side. Unrealistic expectations, unfocused leadership, unclear milestones, lack of interaction, and weak processes within the project team and its management. And don't forget the technology risks of inadequate skills, undefined operations, ineffective design, lack of quality assurance, and technical debt. IT innovation projects give people lots of reasons to be frightened, but as Andy reassures you, risk mitigation is possible.

The following chapters show you many of the ways forward. The detail is impressive and convincing—and obviously hard won.

Chapter 5 covers deal parameters and types of global sourcing arrangements. I especially like the discussion of the trade-offs between cost and quality, in which Andy establishes a $40–$90 per hour sweet spot for enterprise-grade offshore development staff. In a study of 85 global IT sourcing arrangements, my research team and I found inherent problems when the lowest price suppliers were chosen, including serious negative impacts for clients and a winner's curse for suppliers.

Chapter 6 argues for, and demonstrates the importance of, right-fit partners. One sentence shines out for me here: "Only work with partners that are big enough to scale, and small enough to care." The chapter provides a very usable checklist for assessing vendors and their capabilities, and Guest Expert Troy Hiltbrand adds in the vital human dimension by reminding us all that "face to face is where the magic happens."

Chapter 7 provides an illuminating, highly detailed practical section on how to build "One Team." Why is this necessary? Andy is very clear that a lack of cultural or work practice alignment is a major contributor to outsourcing's unenviable failure rate of 25%.

To help you overcome cultural obstacles, Andy shares the steps he takes to help multinational teams optimise performance, including culture mapping, project vision alignment, clearly identified roles and responsibilities, open communications, and more. Guest expert Olivier Poulard observes that "when you can create this same mindset in your in-house and outsourced people, you effectively create what I call a 'oneshore' team of committed developers who respect each other, enjoy working together, and understand that the success of your project is very much in their own self-interest."

Chapters 8 and 9 move the focus on to emerging technologies, their promise, and their management. I particularly enjoyed Chapter 8 on staying relevant with the rise of AI, which is one of my own study areas. Guillermo Kopp told Andy that we're still living in the Bronze Age when it comes to AI, which is just about right. That said, the chapter finds plenty of reason to believe in the future of AI in software development, and I admire Andy's realistic assessment of its promise and challenges.

For Andy, the software developer of the future will need to be adept at the following skills: understanding AI capabilities, defining problem statements, choosing appropriate data, crafting training strategies for AI models, addressing biases and ethical considerations, and continuous learning and adaptation. This is indeed a well-informed, wise steer for future software development professionals and organisations alike.

Like me, a self-confessedly great believer in the things AI cannot do, Rich Mironov has many sensible things to say in Chapter 8's Guest Expert Spotlight, including "I'm not worried about the robots right now because building systems is hard intellectual work that requires real user input, nuanced human interactions, strategic thinking, and empathy…Until they become human they'll simply remain tools that can help humans do important work."

Chapter 9 focuses on the inescapable trend of hyperspecialisation. The demand for innovative and emerging technologies is rising, with key priorities falling in machine learning, natural language processing, cloud computing, robotic process automation (RPA), data science/analytics, Internet of Things (IoT), DevOps, and cybersecurity. The list is always provisional, and that is the challenge.

For Andy, the winning strategy is to identify the technologies that will let you stand out and seek the best expertise to help you realise your vision. The fact is, if you already have a global management mindset, you'll be able to find this expertise more easily than your competitors.

This moves us at last to Chapter 10 and the idea of the tech value network. Andy believes that if you're not currently outsourcing a significant portion of your software development and perfecting the way you manage multinational teams, you'll have a much harder time catching up in the future. He makes a convincing case for the viability and necessity of utilising the business partnering ecosystem approach to leveraging talent globally, backed by proven management skills and an open-mindedness to other cultures.

Synergea reveals the secrets to making this approach work. That it depends much more on people, management, and modes of organising than on technology becomes obvious the closer you get to the subject. That it also depends on the quieter leadership attributes of humility, clarity, experience, and courage, is something that Andy Hilliard exhibits very well indeed.

Leslie Willcocks
Professor of Technology Work and Globalization
London School of Economics

PROLOGUE

Imagine there's no countries
It isn't hard to do…

You may say I'm a dreamer
But I'm not the only one
I hope someday you'll join us
And the world will live as one

—John Lennon

Hundreds of millions of years ago, the 195 countries we know today were all part of a single landmass called Pangea. The name comes from a Greek word meaning "all the Earth."

I often wonder what our world would be like if Pangea hadn't split up and spread out into seven continents. How many different cultures would there be? Where would we find the centers of power and influence? How many languages would people speak? How would trade and communication function across about half as many time zones than the 24 we have today?

While we can never answer these questions, technology is metaphorically pulling the continents back together in some unique and exciting ways. Communication is faster and easier than ever before. International travel is more accessible to more people. And the global economy is breaking down cultural barriers on a daily basis.

With greater synergy worldwide, I'm envisioning a new kind of intellectual supercontinent where people from different countries collaborate to advance shared business goals and create a better world. I can already see it happening in the world of software development, in which the majority of companies outsource at least some of their development and engineering work to people in other countries.

It's an exciting time to be part of this economic movement and I hope you can take advantage of it. This book explores the benefits of expanded outsourcing, offers advice for successfully managing dispersed international teams, and gives you a roadmap for navigating Synergea in our connected global economy. Just imagine the possibilities...

INTRODUCTION

Not too long ago among American businesses, outsourcing was an outlier. Quite naturally, companies in the U.S. didn't want to come under scrutiny for "taking away American jobs." For quite some time, many businesses either refused to consider outsourcing or they did it under the radar.

Even in today's global economy—in which about two-thirds of American businesses send some work to other countries—I still have clients who are uncomfortable with the term "outsourcing" and its connotations. What makes this even more surprising is that I work in technology, an area of business that's even more widely outsourced. According to ISG Research, 92% of G2000 companies use IT outsourcing to cut costs and operate more efficiently.

While people still use the term "outsourcing" to search for companies like Accelerance, the company I lead, people I engage with prefer terms like "multi-partner sourcing," "multinational management," or "distributed team management." I admit I like these terms, too, because they speak to the cooperative spirit involved in making the kind of software development projects we specialize in a success. The term "outsourcing" is rather clinical, when it's really all about diverse groups of people working well together to achieve a common goal.

Whatever you want to call it, the whole point of this book is to help you find the best people around the world so you can create high performing environments. If you're in technology, product development, or operations, I'll be sharing insights that apply directly to this value chain. But even if you don't work in these areas, you'll gain a greater understanding of what it takes to manage people across time zones, geographies, and cultures.

The last few years have accelerated the relevance of the multinational management model, which is one that my team at Accelerance has been perfecting behind the scenes for more than two decades. Now that it's taking center stage and becoming more of a strategic imperative for businesses of all sizes and across all industries, you'll need to get up to speed quickly so you can manage people on site, nearshore, and offshore as one cohesive team.

This book reveals many of the valuable lessons we've learned about effective multinational management over the years, which I hope you can use to build more effective teams and gain competitive advantage.

My experiences in the Peace Corps opened my eyes to the value of cross-cultural cooperation.

My particular interest in outsourcing and multinational management stems from my experiences in the Peace Corps as a young man. Three or four years out of college I had a quarter-life crisis. I was working at a big bank in Colorado, but it wasn't my calling and I knew I needed to shake things up in a dramatic way. I was ready for something truly life changing.

On a cross-country skiing trip one weekend, a friend of mine told me about his two-year experience on a kibbutz in Israel. His story took on extra meaning and magic as the snow blended with the stars on a crisp Rocky Mountain night among the tall conifers, and I was literally transfixed.

Shortly thereafter, I landed a microenterprise development assignment in Costa Rica through the Peace Corps. My experience as a commercial lender was exactly what they were looking for, and I was on my way to the safe and beautiful country known as the Switzerland of Central America.

Costa Rica is everything it's cracked up to be, with its magnificent volcanoes and cloud forests, spectacular sandy beaches, and rich biodiversity. But it was really the people there that impressed me the most. Most everyone spoke some English, each person I encountered greeted me with warmth and authenticity, and the team members I worked with as a Small Enterprise Consultant were all hard-working and eager to hone their crafts, improve their lives, and support their loved ones.

I was based in Santa Cruz, Guanacaste, a town of about 5,000 people in the Pacific Northwest region of the country. My small, one-bedroom house was made from cement and had a tin roof, and my work involved helping fishing cooperatives and ceramics associations become more profitable. It wasn't a glamorous life, but it had an integrity and authenticity about it that was hard to beat.

When I wasn't working, I soaked in the local culture, spending most of my free time coaching baseball, teaching English, hanging out with my neighbors, and admiring the relaxed Costa Rican way of living. A few weeks into my stay I built a gym in my backyard and brought in bars, plates, benches, and dumbbells. Kids in the neighborhood would come over and we'd all work out together, and it really became the focal point for a rich cultural exchange.

Meeting my soulmate in Costa Rica kept my ties to the country strong.

I was even fortunate enough to meet the woman who would become my wife. Silvia, the youngest of 11 kids, was an administrator for the Peace Corps and I'd see her once a month when I had to go to the office in the capital for a program review and a health check. When I left the Peace Corps to go to business school, she told me that if I really wanted to marry her I'd come back over Christmas, which I did. Fortunately, she said yes.

With Silvia's family in Costa Rica, my ties to the country have remained strong over the years—through business school, during my time as a brand manager for Nestle, through another stint as a banker, and while I was finally finding my calling in multinational management, or outsourcing.

*****

The same friend who inspired me to join the Peace Corps was working at a Dun & Bradstreet spinoff called Cognizant, a fast-growing technology services and consulting firm that was sourcing software development and computer programming talent from India for large American companies. He convinced me to join him there, and during my two years at Cognizant I saw it grow from 700 programmers to more than 20,000. It was clear to me, in the early 2000s, that outsourced software development was the way of the future.

As Cognizant focused more exclusively on enterprise, Fortune 1000 clients, I saw an opportunity to offer similar services to small and medium-sized businesses. On a trip back to Costa Rica to see my wife's family, I met with executives at several software development companies and ended up buying into one of them. My intention was to bring them U.S.-based clients who wouldn't qualify or be able to work effectively with India for various reasons, such as time zone incompatibility, distance, and cultural misalignment.

In 2003, I co-founded a nearshore software development company, Isthmus Costa Rica, which was totally focused on providing software engineering services to U.S. clients. It was quite possibly the first company to completely dedicate itself to the U.S. market, and we distinguished ourselves by providing English fluency throughout the organization (Costa Rica remains number one in English fluency due to economic and political alignment with the U.S.), access to the best graduates and professionals in the market, ISO and CMMI certifications, up-to-date security protocols, and a U.S.-based leadership presence.

That same year, I met serial entrepreneur and management thought leader Steve Mezak at a globalization conference. He was writing his seminal book on outsourcing at the time, *Software without Borders: A Step-By-Step Guide to Outsourcing Your Software Development*. Originally published in 2006, the book remains a relevant primer for learning the right ways to make software development outsourcing work.

I told Steve that I could be the poster boy for his thesis that there's great development talent everywhere, not just in India, because I was taking the best practices I learned from my tenure at Cognizant and using them to create a new business model for small and medium-sized businesses.

We hit it off right away and continued to feed off each other. He crafted content and thought leadership based on my experiences in the field.

Isthmus had grown from zero to 300 developers by 2007, and we were doing amazing work for companies like TSYS, DHL, Gannett, and Ariba.

The company is still going strong today, but I sold my shares back to Isthmus in 2009 when I chose to partner with Steve in Accelerance, a business he had started in 2001. Our goal together was to develop a fully vetted, trustworthy, and certified global network of software development providers for small and mid-sized U.S. businesses. We added value by mitigating the risks of outsourcing, helping our clients safely and smartly leverage the same benefits—talent, skills, lower costs, and best practices—that were really only feasible for large companies working with blue chip global development groups.

The perception at the time was that outsourcing was dangerous, especially for smaller organizations that couldn't afford to absorb the shock of an expensive, high-profile failure. Many companies were burned by outsourcing partners who just wanted to make fast money by capitalizing on the trend. Others had bad experiences in the Indian market because it was too far away, and all the focused attention and VIP treatment went to larger clients.

Steve and I worked hard to make outsourcing easy for the companies that partnered with us, because we saw that ever-increasing globalization and digitalization were making multinational management of software development projects a necessity for businesses of all sizes.

*****

The evolution toward outsourcing skills and services to talent-laden, lower-cost regions began after World War II, when business practitioners like IBM and GE saw the financial benefits of conducting certain activities in markets where labor was less expensive.

While some hurdles had to be overcome—such as cultural differences, time zone confusion, inefficient or expensive communication methods, and the cost of shipping products over great distances—the tradeoffs could still work in a business's favor.

As technology advanced, it became easier to connect with people anywhere in the world. Other business functions beyond manufacturing became ripe for outsourcing, most notably call center operations and software development. Indian companies, including Tata, Infosys, and Wipro, were formed and thrived by providing highly skilled, low-cost services to clients like Dell, Intel, and Cisco in high-cost, low talent-supply locations.

In the 1990s and early 2000s, around the time I started working at Cognizant, people started talking about "strategic" outsourcing. Unlike traditional outsourcing, which is purely transactional for reducing the cost of simple tasks requiring no specialized skills, strategic outsourcing adds on the idea of tapping into external expertise that can help a company gain a competitive advantage.

Indian programmers were in such high demand in the mid 1990s and early 2000s for many reasons, including the simple fact that so many of them were available. Government officials and business leaders throughout India saw the potential of the emerging technology industry to lift a significant percentage of the population out of poverty, so they cleared pathways for educational opportunities and work experience.

When the earliest tech startups began commercializing the Internet, India was ready and willing to help them minimize the risk with an inexpensive, skilled talent pool that spoke English and could keep development work going around the clock. Demand for talent from India increased as the Internet took off, and Indian engineers and developers carried Western tech companies through the entire dot-com boom. They even did the lion's share of the legacy code reviews and updates that were necessitated by the Y2K scare, and to this day they remain a powerful force in the technology industry. Nearly six million developers are employed in India today, more than any other country.

The digital transformation that began in the mid-1990s ultimately led us to where we are today, with "transformational" outsourcing attracting the attention of folks in C-suites across the country. Viewed through this more expansive lens, outsourcing becomes a mandatory prerequisite for greater agility, faster innovation, and sustainable growth.

While we likely would have gotten to this point eventually, we know all too well that a dramatic sea change occurred in 2020 that accelerated the process. COVID-19 forced pretty much all businesses to rapidly shift to the principles and models that have defined outsourcing's organic evolution over the past decades.

And once business leaders got comfortable working with distributed teams of their own, many were awakened to this glorious epiphany:

When workers are untethered from specific locations, organizations can find the best talent from anywhere.

This liberating idea—which took many businesses out of an entrenched, all-my-eggs-in-one-basket mentality—opened people's eyes to the value of new ways of working in a global economy.

Aravinda Gollapudi, Head of Platform and Technology at Sage, for example, told us in 2021 that "the notion of how we generally operate...has changed...We didn't have to hire in high-cost regions such as the Bay Area anymore. We were able to go hire in lower-cost markets, such as Atlanta. Even in India, we hired people in more remote locations with good colleges...and talent pools."

*****

In my role as CEO of one of the premier global software development outsourcing advisories, I've seen businesses of all kinds benefit from embracing a multinational management model for a wide variety of digital transformation projects.

- **Fintech firms** are using multinational teams to develop innovative solutions that power and maintain digital banking, payments, and custodial platforms. Through software development outsourcing, an industry known for slow decision making and strict security requirements is learning how to modernize and innovate.

- **Medical device manufacturers** are using multinational technology teams to support critical research and development. Not only does this reduce overall costs and financial risk, but it also generates faster turnarounds and frees up in-house resources. To succeed in today's competitive environment, companies in this sector are feeling the pressure to develop better products more quickly, while controlling costs at the same time.

- **Consumer packaged goods companies** are using multinational teams to meet product development needs, create richer product pipelines, and run multiple projects simultaneously.

The list goes on and on. Strategically looking beyond borders provides a jump start to companies in all industries that want to ramp up innovation and operational efficiency. A multinational, employee-statusless approach to projects facilitates access to the most technology-forward capabilities available and is more scalable and cost-effective than an internal build could ever be.

When a company wants (or needs) to grow, embracing multinational management facilitates the acquisition of fresh development skills and expertise from a global talent pool, often at a significantly lower cost.

Businesses of all sizes recognize the need to maneuver with speed and agility in today's fast-paced, technology-driven global economy. They understand that digital transformation is the name of the game. And whether a company is building a cloud-based application from scratch, scaling up teams to finish a backlog of projects, integrating IT departments after a merger, or planning to increase development capacity, velocity, and cost-effectiveness, they often need to cast a wider net to find the expertise they need to stay competitive.

The appetite for digital transformation and cloud migration projects that improve efficiency and enhance the customer experience has never been stronger, which puts an even greater strain on available resources and expertise.

Without a multinational management strategy, chief technology officers, chief product officers, and chief operating officers commonly lose sleep over slipping timelines, idle resources, and rising costs, with prospects of project failures always looming in the background.

Business leaders are fast coming to the realization that they have nothing to lose and everything to gain by learning how to manage multinational teams. While we'll go into the benefits of this new business paradigm in more detail throughout this book, I'll just say now that if you bring this model into your organization you'll be handsomely rewarded in four key areas:

1. **Cost Savings**
   Application developers, especially those with the most prized skills, are extremely expensive. As IT executives look to reduce costs, hiring development and engineering talent in lower-cost locations makes more sense.

2. **Demand Management**
   The need for specific technical skills varies significantly as business conditions change and technology advances. As IT initiatives scale up and down, the willingness and ability to manage multinational teams can keep you gracefully in sync with fluctuating demand.

3. **Skills Sourcing**
   To keep pace with digital transformation, companies are bolstering in-house resources with uniquely skilled developers worldwide. These days, the best talent is often located outside the United States.

4. Investment

Application development, often IT's largest line item, will continue to command a bigger share of tech budgets as the innovation agenda remains a top priority.

Now is the time to get the fundamentals of multinational management right, fine-tune your structures and pricing models, and create a cost-effective network of top practitioners you can call upon when needed.

More and more, I see the proliferation of hybrid teams made up of in-house staff and contracted outsourcing partners. This type of staff configuration enables companies to keep momentum going by rapidly filling capacity—and capability—gaps. Multi-partner, multinational management is fast becoming the new norm, as businesses work to future-proof operations through the creation of worldwide tech value networks, whose members can be called upon to provide the right skills at the right time. It's getting to the point where organizations that don't embrace multinational management models will be left in the dust.

The Software Outsourcing Lifecycle

In the pages that follow, I'll essentially take you through the stages of the software outsourcing lifecycle, so you can learn how to make the theory—including the management of culturally blended, international teams—work in practice for your organization.

Along the way, I'll share stories from some of our clients and partners, as well as best practices for making sure you're ready to optimize every stage:

Planning
You'll learn how to make sure that your business is ready for multinational management success. Since most projects fail because of internal weaknesses, doing the appropriate prep work will make it much easier for you to avoid problems and resolve issues once you decide to take the plunge.

Partner Selection
Evaluating outsourcing partners, especially since an increasing number of fly-by-night organizations are popping up to make a quick buck, requires a balance of thorough due diligence and fast action. I'll outline the categories you need to cover to choose the perfect partners, and I'll give you specific questions to ask in each category. This information has been distilled down from my team's own proprietary vetting process, which measures the capabilities of software development firms against more than 500 separate criteria.

Onboarding
Once you choose a partner, the real work begins. To help you successfully navigate the onboarding process, I'll show you how to embrace your newly blended team, create a shared vision, and establish open communication channels and effective workflow. I'll share the secrets we reveal to our clients in the intensive, three-day alignment workshops we conduct with them to generate positive momentum at the start of every project.

Operation
And lastly, I'll give you valuable tips and techniques for making sure your blended, international team performs at a high level throughout your engagement. Armed with this information, you'll deliver the

kind of results that will make you a hero for suggesting that some of your development work should be outsourced.

Once you have some success with outsourcing and multinational management, you'll see firsthand the value it can bring to your organization. It's my goal to lead you on a path that takes you from considering outsourcing as a tactic to realizing its strategic power as a driver of organizational growth.

I'll close this introduction with a few notes about the human side of multinational management that aren't talked about enough in corporate America. In the Peace Corps, two of our three goals were unrelated to whatever projects we were working on. One of these goals was to share our culture with others and have them appreciate where we came from, and the other was to learn about their culture and share it with people back home.

Breaking down stereotypes, being open to new experiences, and finding common ground in pursuit of a shared purpose are all incredibly rewarding experiences—personally as well as professionally.

And, for those of us with an unquenchable thirst for adventure—or even those with a mild curiosity about different cultures—it doesn't hurt being able to take a few days enjoying the natural beauty, bustling cities, and other attractions of places like Costa Rica, Peru, Hungary, Slovenia, Sri Lanka, Vietnam, or Egypt after meeting or celebrating with your teammates.

Multinational management will transform your organization, and it may just transform your life if you let it.

"The only thing that will redeem mankind is cooperation."
—*Bertrand Russell*

CHAPTER 1

DISRUPTION 101: EXPECT THE UNEXPECTED

If there's one thing we can all be certain about in business, it's uncertainty. From natural disasters and geopolitical conflicts to economic downturns and talent shortages, we never quite know what's going to happen next.

Who among us, in the fall of 2019, could have predicted that within six months a pandemic would turn the entire world upside down, force a global workforce out of the office, and change how we think about remote employees for the rest of our lives?

Today, we find ourselves with global talent resources at our disposal unlike any other time in our history. Businesses that seize the opportunities this new reality provides will go a long way toward future-proofing their operations.

The trick—which is the whole point of this book—is to learn how to tap into the right talent pools at the right times and manage the people you bring on from anywhere in the world as if they were part of your in-house team. If you figure out how to do this well, you'll be much less likely to become a victim of external forces that can slow down your growth, inflate your budgets, and erode your market share.

What kind of external forces am I talking about? You can find a lot of them in something called the Emerging Risks Report, which is published quarterly by Gartner. Based on surveys and conversations with risk professionals and managers around the globe, the report identifies issues related to economics, technology, talent, climate, and politics that could have a negative business impact.

Reading this report is not for the faint of heart. You'll find lots of things to worry about, such as stagflation and rising costs in North America, currency volatility in Asia, the impact of geopolitical conflicts on energy markets, and other doomsday scenarios that could wreak havoc on your business. Every quarter, it's a different horror story!

While it's important to keep things in perspective and not panic about every potential problem, we can't just put our heads in the sand and pretend that the world isn't a complex place with lots of different variables. It's good to know what we should have on our radar, and the more educated we are about the issues that could impact our livelihoods, the better prepared we'll be to avoid sticky situations or, at minimum, weather the various storms better than our competitors.

I keep telling people how important it is to adopt a management model that lets them pivot as quickly as possible when conditions change—for better or for worse. Whether you're trying to solve a problem or capitalize on an unexpected opportunity, the early bird is the one who catches the worm. No matter how drastically conditions change, your goals are always the same—keep productivity high, keep costs low, and meet or exceed the demands of your customers and shareholders.

Ria Delamere is one of my clients who had an interesting thing happen when the pandemic hit—demand for her company's online learning programs for employees went through the roof! "The edtech market exploded," she told me. "It escalated everything so fast that it made our three-to-four-year plans almost imminent."

While this was a good problem to have, her company—Open Sesame—had to act quickly to meet the sudden spike in demand. While the pandemic presented its own set of challenges around fulfilling this need, the business was also affected by the Great Resignation. Just when Ria needed people the most, she had difficulty finding them.

With our help, Ria, whose role is Vice President of Engineering, hired developers in Mexico and Ukraine and tripled her engineering team in a year and a half. "I used to think that we had to source engineering out of the U.S. because it's easier to manage," she said. "Now that we've opened our doors we definitely operate with a remote-first mindset."

Having that kind of openness and flexibility has been serving Ria and her company quite well. Expanding her team internationally wasn't without its share of stress, but it was the answer the company needed to get its educational products into the eager hands of a whole new audience.

Ria and her team at Open Sesame are constantly learning, improving, and adapting. When the war in Ukraine began, doors to her contacts there closed very quickly and she had to look for new opportunities to hire people in the Baltics, Poland, and other adjacent European markets, in addition to additional locations in Latin America.

Keep Innovating—No Matter What

I love Ria because she's always looking for ways to make lemonade when the world throws lemons at her. Her advice to business leaders is to keep innovating, even when the economy shows ominous signs.

"You never want to take your foot off the gas because it takes a long while to ramp up and get those efficiencies back," she said. "I think it's better to lean into the momentum because you might be able to pick up better resources than you could have before."

Outsourcing Success Story: A Wartime Workaround

Mark Stewart faced a CTO's nightmare: War broke out when a Ukrainian team was his sole support for developing an advanced back-office software platform for real estate professionals. Mark needed backup resources ASAP, but they had to have highly specialized skills that were difficult to come by—and they needed to be able to hit the ground running.

Against all odds, Mark came to us for help. "Within a couple days, we had three strong contenders and we were interviewing them within a week," he recalls. "It was all very easy for us, even though we were searching for a needle in a haystack." One of our certified partners in Brazil came through with a team of six developers who were skilled in the Ruby programming language and the Flutter framework.

As the conflict in Ukraine escalated, Mark's new Brazilian team needed to start working with his in-house people immediately. We accelerated team onboarding and integration through an intensive three-day Zoom workshop, which covered cultural differences, workflow expectations, communication protocols, and what success around a shared vision looked like (more on this in Chapter 7).

During the workshop, everyone on the blended team got to practice working together. "It was definitely valuable to get the teams up and running quickly and to establish their working norms," Mark remembers. "The new team really got off on the right foot."

Mark was able to stand up an entirely new team of skilled developers within a month, but the payoff was much longer lasting: He now has another outsourcing team—from a more stable world region—that he can rely on for key application support.

Aravinda Gollapudi, the leader at Sage I mentioned earlier, agrees with Ria and even used the same metaphor. "Innovation is the one thing where we will not take the foot off the pedal," she told us in an interview. "The world is moving very quickly. We can't afford to ramp down."

Build Your Business Resilience

A focus on continuous innovation can be a driving force in the face of change and disruption because innovation is inherently disruptive by itself. Being an innovator puts you in the right mindset—in fact, it allows you to welcome change because you're creating it anyway.

But you also must work hard to build your business resilience at all times. Even when things are going well and running smoothly, you need plans in place to help you deal with the unknown. How confident are you that you can stay one step ahead of the next crisis? Will you pivot or panic when the next problem arises?

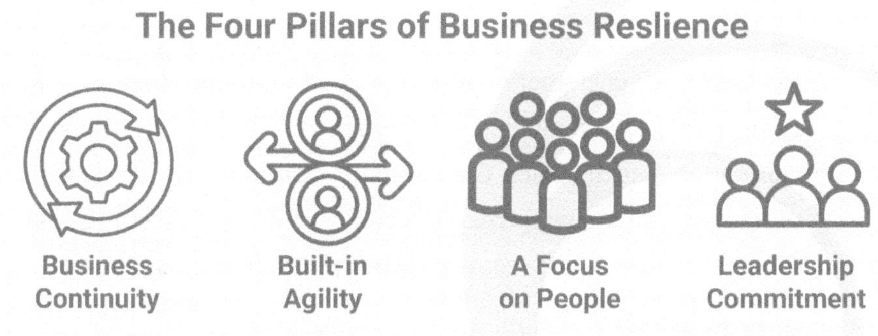

To keep things simple, I like to boil business resilience down to four overlapping components: business continuity, built-in agility, a focus on people, and leadership commitment.

All these pillars can and should be studied, researched, and formalized at your organization, but if you haven't figured me out already, I prefer to learn by doing. So, I'm going to breeze through these ideas to give you some context, and then I'm going to show you how embracing a multinational management model naturally puts theory into practice and helps you prepare for just about any possibility.

As we go through the pillars, keep in mind that even though I'm talking about catastrophic situations, the ideas apply to smaller issues that can arise on a daily basis. It's just as important to have business resilience when dealing with minor problems as it is to have business resilience when it comes to major issues. If you can't tackle things early, they have the potential to balloon into something bigger, and much less manageable, later.

So here we go, a quick summary of the key components of business resilience:

1. **Business Continuity**
   As I mentioned earlier, your goal is to keep functioning as best as you can through a crisis, serving your clients, operating your core platforms, and selling your goods or services. Keeping things going can mean opening new digital channels, relying on more remote workers, or tapping into a data backup if your information is corrupted or compromised.

   Because your customers will likely need you more than ever in a crisis, they just assume that you have the foresight to put a business continuity plan in place that formally assesses risks, establishes mitigation strategies, increases security, and has protocols in place for responding to, and recovering from, different threats.

2. **Built-in Agility**
   If you can't mobilize your people and assets quickly to adapt to a new operating environment, you'll be left behind by your customers and competitors alike.

   You must have agility ingrained into your organization's culture and processes to rapidly respond to challenges. If you're confident in your business continuity planning, you'll have an easier time making critical decisions in the face of an emerging crisis. How long will it take to stand up new e-commerce services? Can you rewrite your applications to meet new public safety regulations? Will your customers be left stranded in a tough situation, or will you win their loyalty by continuing to serve them? An agile approach will give you the confidence and grace you need to work well under pressure.

3. **A Focus on People**

   People power agility. Chris Ruch, who runs a company I really like called Agile Rising, says that "companies need to move beyond a culture of process adherence to one of self-discipline, freedom, responsibility, and service to customers." Empowering people is necessary for developing a resilient workforce and creating effective teams whose members work well—together and individually—to achieve a shared purpose.

   Chris believes that "agility is about collaborating, iterating, and getting feedback." These human actions are much more effective when team members trust each other, respect each other, and are genuinely interested in the unique perspectives everyone brings to the table. In my view, this is the true value of diversity.

4. **Leadership Commitment**

   A commitment to fostering resilience needs to start at the top of your organization and permeate the business. This requires championing—and modeling—a vision of excellence, innovation, and teamwork that empowers people to embrace agility and do their best, even when problems occur. If your leaders can pivot and not panic, everyone else in your organization will be more likely to do the same.

   This aspect of business resilience requires continuous energy, foresight, and a willingness to assign resources now to ensure future success. To varying degrees, these are the activities your business leaders should always be working on:

- Understanding and prioritizing risks that might impact your business
- Monitoring your industry and world events, especially in places where you operate facilities or distribute products
- Developing a business continuity plan and keeping it up to date
- Encouraging a culture of innovation that welcomes new ideas, perspectives, and approaches
- Training your people so they can grow the business by growing themselves
- Facilitating collaboration, especially across functions

If your leaders advocate for these actions consistently, your teams will not only be able to function well when the inevitable disruptions occur, but they'll also create a company that people will love working at no matter what market conditions are like.

*****

The beauty of a multinational management model is that it gives you automatic business resilience and lets you practice the four pillars that make your business resilience muscles stronger.

Right off the bat, you'll gain the peace of mind that comes from knowing you can find people with the skills you need somewhere in the world. It's especially satisfying when you can easily access people with skills that are hard to find locally—and pay a lot less for them!

Once you get comfortable with the process and start expanding your trusted network, you'll feel even more reassured that you can put the exact resources you need in place without delay. Most of our clients aren't always managing multinational teams, but they know they can ramp up that capability whenever they need to.

Having the ability to effectively manage distributed teams is clearly a way to enhance business continuity and agility, and it really puts an emphasis on the "focus on people" pillar of business resilience. Diverse, multinational teams are tremendous sources of fresh ideas, perspectives, and approaches—and potential innovations.

Harnessing the creative power of people from different cultures—who all want the same results you do—will literally do incredible things for your business. We've really gotten to the point where world-class talent can be sourced from anywhere, and it amazes me that so many of our clients are still surprised by this. The majority of people we work with come into outsourcing with low expectations, which I guess is a good thing because once they start working on projects they're thrilled by the level of quality they get.

The world has changed dramatically, and the U.S. is no longer the only place you can find people who can deliver an innovative, market-leading solution. Pockets of greatness are everywhere, and it's worth it to go looking for them. In fact, it's really not that hard to beat some of the development companies operating in the U.S. right now by going nearshore or offshore.

We recently worked with a financial services client that wanted to develop a new product that could automate audit processes. It was a very large and complex strategic initiative that our client was investing in, and they wanted an outsourced development team to work with their in-house financial and business process experts. We helped them find a team of 30 developers and engineers with a partner in Brazil that blew our client away with their innovative methods around design thinking. The approach was unlike anything our client had ever seen before, and the excitement it generated won the deal for the Brazilian firm.

As huge a win as it was for our Brazilian partner—I'm talking three or four million dollars in revenue over several years—our client saved about 40% off what it would have cost them if they hired local talent. This was definitely a win-win situation, and it opened our client's eyes to the idea that excellence can come from unexpected places.

I can come up with countless examples of how innovation can be led by mature and experienced teams from anywhere in the world. So many people outside the U.S., based on education and experience, are qualified to deliver work of a standard suitable for Western markets. One of the partner firms we work with in Pakistan, for instance, is run by a group of people who all graduated from Stanford University and now teach at the university level. If they wanted to live in America they'd be here, but they've chosen instead to go back to their home country.

We're seeing lots of this type of movement as older developers and engineers return to the countries of their birth to care for aging parents. One of our partners in California has found great success finding outsourcing jobs for developers and engineers who studied and worked in the U.S. and have recently moved back to India.

Nowadays, all companies can hire world-class software development talent in countries like Brazil, Pakistan, and India. Far too many, however, choose instead to hire someone in San Diego, Raleigh, or Boston for a lot more money. That person might do an okay job, but the company that's doing the hiring is truly missing an opportunity to work with someone who could add an extra layer of innovation, deliver a rich cultural experience, and enhance the organization's overall business resilience.

*****

Companies that outsourced at least part of their software development to global partners before the pandemic hit were among those that best absorbed the economic shock of the COVID-19 disruption. These companies had the fewest logistical challenges because they already knew how remote working worked. They were prepared for the pandemic—even though they weren't planning for it—and they didn't have to scramble like everyone else did. In many ways, it was business as usual for these companies because they had the business resilience they needed to meet changing conditions without missing a beat.

Today, more and more businesses are realizing the need to prepare for future disruption. Fortunately, the near-universal acceptance of remote working has gone a long way toward helping companies become more resilient and use geographically dispersed teams to add value.

As more companies have expanded their outsourcing engagements over the past several years, we're learning that the sweet spot for mitigating geographic risk, expanding your talent pool, lowering costs, and gaining other benefits of business resilience is to outsource between 25 and 75 percent of your software development.

For many of our clients, this is an easy goal to achieve. They may start with one in-house development team, for example, and just by adding another one in a different country they're suddenly outsourcing 50 percent of their work. While this provides a cushion against disruption, I believe it's important to have outsourcing partners—or at least access to outsourcing partners—in multiple locations for true business resilience. It doesn't have to happen right away, but if you're going to make a commitment to managing multinational teams you should have that goal in mind as you go along.

In the next chapter, we'll briefly explore the changes that have made remote work the new status quo for many organizations and discuss a few more benefits of business without borders.

GUEST EXPERT SPOTLIGHT

JEFF SHUPACK

Digital transformation and business agility consultant Jeff Shupack currently serves as Executive Board Member & President of Advisory Practice for Project & Team. The global consultancy helps Fortune 100 companies and government agencies take a culture-based approach to digital transformation that's underpinned by the proven practices of Scaled Agile Framework (SAFe), Lean-Agile, Industrial DevOps, Digital Engineering, and Design Thinking.

The Most Dramatic Disruptions Are Happening Within

Old ways of working are among the biggest barriers to business resilience.

The speed of market disruption is increasing, forcing businesses to adapt more quickly than ever if they want to stay competitive. To effectively create new opportunities for growth and innovation, organizations must be willing to embrace internal disruption in two important ways. First, by becoming learning organizations that use data to drive decisions. And second, by letting go of old ways of doing things that are incompatible with how uncertainty and change need to be dealt with today.

It's clear that whoever learns how to overcome obstacles the fastest is going to be the most competitive. In my practice, which has been dedicated to helping company executives transform their organizations, it's been exciting to realize that the basic principles of Agile software development can be applied throughout the enterprise: iterate often, fail fast, and learn from your mistakes. This virtuous learning loop results in faster time-to-market, improved productivity, exceptional customer focus, and empowering environments where people want to work.

Try these three things to facilitate your own transformation and you'll be amazed by the results:

1. Stop organizing in functional silos
2. Keep effective, cross-functional teams together and move work to them
3. Provide your people with intent—and get out of the way

Scaling team capacities by working with external partners—in software development and beyond—is the first step in being able to adapt to disruption. Multinational management is gaining momentum because it requires lean and agile thinking around people, teams, and ultimately teams of teams that are working globally to achieve critical business objectives.

But gaining access to more people with the right technical capabilities is only half the battle. You must also upskill your internal and external people to a different way of working that decentralizes decision making and trusts in the fact that most people want to add value.

The way I look at it is that there's no such thing as outsourcing anymore: For businesses that want to scale, there's no other way to do business than through multinational teams that stick together and ignore the concepts of FTEs, vendors, and partners. You absolutely want everyone on your teams—local and remote—to be treated the same exact way or you're not going to get the innovative, market-leading solutions you're looking for.

Leaders need to accept the fact that past management frameworks aren't working in the age of digital and AI. If we could accurately measure the organizational debt created by outdated ways of working, it would truly be astonishing. Traditional silos pit people against each other and make business resilience harder to achieve. A better approach is to gather everyone involved in the development of a solution, let them know what needs to be accomplished, and give them the freedom to figure it out together. You can keep your hierarchies for certain strategic decisions, but day-to-day decisions should be decentralized as much as possible.

You can reduce risk and create a better way of working if you're willing to encourage experimentation, create an environment of rapid learning (a task that can be automated in exciting ways with new data-centric and AI operating architectures), and focus on fast, elegant recovery when things get disrupted. That's the Agile Manifesto across the enterprise: What are the best experiments you can run to get the best and fastest feedback? How can you measure results against expected economic outcomes? How can you regroup from mistakes?

Assuming you'll get a lot of things wrong and embracing the inevitability of disruption changes your whole mindset. Instead of beating people up for mistakes, you learn from them and try to get things right the next time. And because an answer that's right today may be wrong tomorrow, changing your mindset enables continuous adaptation to market dynamics and other forces.

Far too often, outdated behaviors from leadership erode what's best for the business. The next generation of workers want a different type of structure. The world of software development and engineering is unique because most of the practitioners are in their twenties and thirties. They learn differently, process information at higher speeds, and are comfortable using an evolving set of tools that are thrown away every couple of months for something better.

Google did hundreds of interviews across its own organization and found that "who" is on a team matters less than "how" team members interact with each other, structure their work, and view their contributions to the overall effort. In other words, it all comes down to team dynamics. In performance-oriented organizations it just doesn't matter if team members are contractors, consultants, or employees. Leaders in these organizations just want high functioning teams that are constantly learning, innovating, and producing real value through economic outcomes.

For the best way to handle disruption a new leadership approach is desperately needed, one that channels cross-functional collaboration and makes everyone feel valued and empowered. As famed engineer, author, and management consultant W. Edwards Deming once said, "A system must be managed. It will not manage itself. Left to themselves, components become selfish, competitive, independent profit centers, and thus destroy the system. The secret is cooperation between components toward the aim of the organization."

"The world is one country and mankind its citizens."
——*Bahá'u'lláh*

CHAPTER 2

BUSINESS WITHOUT BORDERS: THE OFFICE WILL NEVER BE THE SAME AGAIN

If we can say that anything good came out of the pandemic, the acceptance of virtual working models—and the accompanying digital transformation—may just be the silver lining of the proverbial cloud.

Now that we've had some time to step back from the fire drill that forced a distributed team management model on companies before anyone could really think about it, we're in a position to learn from what happened and take a more strategic, process-oriented approach to remote work. Even though some companies are pressuring workers to go back to the office, the cat is out of the bag and most businesses are settling on some kind of hybrid or remote-first approach.

In the beginning, when the mad scramble to set up remote teams was happening in real time, corporate executives worried that loose and unstructured working conditions would lead to reductions in productivity. How could you make sure employees were doing their jobs from home when they could be so easily distracted by naps, pets, children, television, social media, the refrigerator, and all the other temptations?

Those of us who've been working with distributed teams for decades, however, knew that the opposite would be true. It's been proven time and time again that remote teams perform just as well, or better, than traditional teams in a single location—and they spend less time around the proverbial water cooler.

Workers are less stressed when they have more freedom and autonomy—not to mention the luxury of avoiding a crowded commute every day—and this translates into greater efficiency, productivity, and satisfaction. Most employees enjoy working remotely, at least some of the time. In one study, a full quarter of respondents said they'd take a 10% pay cut to keep working from home.

In addition to happier, healthier, and more productive workers, employers who embrace a remote-first working model benefit from lower staff turnover, lower overhead, and greater flexibility when it comes to searching for new and additional talent. Global Workplace Analytics, for example, estimates savings of $11,000 a year for every employee who works remotely even half the time.

Remote Workers and Multinational Management

I have a hunch that most of the content in this chapter isn't news to you. Chances are pretty good that you were forced—or chose—to work at home during 2020 and beyond. If you've been part of a remote team, or if you've had to manage a team that found itself working remotely, you've likely gotten many valuable insights you can apply to the management of multinational teams.

Setting cultural issues aside for the time being, all the other aspects of team management are essentially the same:

- How do you align team members on a shared purpose?
- How do you define roles and responsibilities?
- How do you hold team members accountable?
- How do you facilitate collaboration, cooperation, and innovation?
- How do you make each team member feel valued?
- How do you support team members who are struggling?

If you've gained any proficiency with digital tools such as Zoom, Slack, Teams, and Asana, then you've already established a great foundation for managing teams with widely dispersed members. The more practice you've gotten working with (or managing) a formerly in-house team that's become a remote team, the better off you'll be when you add international team members into the mix.

This is such an exciting time for outsourcing, and software development outsourcing in particular, because remote working has been normalized and managers have gotten much better at helping team members work effectively and efficiently without being face-to-face.

According to a 2022 study published by the Association for Talent Development, 69% of managers were overseeing a hybrid team after the pandemic, compared to just 20% prior to the outbreak of COVID-19. The same study reported that 34% of organizations project an increase in the use of hybrid teams, largely because they deliver higher productivity.

Outsourcing Success Story: "Swallowing the Watermelon"

Accelerance client Mike Williamson is the Vice President of Research and Development at Softdocs, an innovative company that makes business process and document management software for educational institutions. Mike is someone who understands the value of being able to add remote workers to his teams when he needs them.

This kind of rapid scalability is something Mike calls "swallowing the watermelon," but it's not nearly as painful as it sounds. As a guy who likes to be creative with his words, Mike also refers to hiring just-in-time, remote resources as "burst capability," which allows him to take advantage of opportunities and respond to challenges as they arise.

Mike uses several nearshoring partners to hire skilled workers that can build new product features and operational functionality for his software. "We can quickly supplement our team with outsourced partner resources or reduce the team size if needed," Mike says. "It helps because we can scale up or down as conditions change."

Maintaining Momentum

Thanks to the success of the nearly universal transition to remote working, CIOs and other IT executives are leveraging their elevated profiles to maintain the momentum of digital business acceleration and globally distributed team management models.

With roadblocks removed, smart businesses are making strategic investments in collaboration tools and worldwide talent recruitment that increase competitiveness and profitability by accelerating product development cycles and facilitating continuous innovation.

Hiring the most talented people and empowering them to innovate pays tremendous dividends. Using video conferencing, messaging, and project management tools—as well as competitive hackathons and preplanned live events—organizations that boost their investment in innovation are nearly three times more likely to be top performers.

Some of the managers I talk with still lament the loss of informal, face-to-face interactions that can often lead to breakthrough ideas, and this is understandable. It might take a while for some people to get over this mindset, especially if they have fond memories of successful, impromptu work interactions. I do believe that once managers and team members get comfortable with remote collaboration, the upside from working with world-class talent in remote locations will more than make up for any downside that may occur from an inability to bump into someone in the hallway or pop into someone's office unannounced.

The key to multinational management success is the ability to find talent with the high-level, specialized expertise required to generate breakthrough ideas. Eighty percent of technology professionals consider digital transformation to be critical to their long-term business viability. And almost two-thirds acknowledge that, to effectively deliver innovation, their internal resources require enhanced expertise and resources from external partners, such as IT outsourcing firms.

What the pandemic has proven is that remote work and managing distributed teams is a viable paradigm for most businesses. And when company leaders realize how valuable the removal of geographic constraints can be in terms of access to great minds and expertise, they rarely look back.

Yogish Suvarna, CIO of Aspen Dental, told *The National CIO Review* that "one of the biggest challenges that every technology leader faces is sourcing the right talent at the right time to meet the constantly changing needs of the business...My advice is to surround yourself with innovative companies and partners who can help you and your team with meeting business needs and bridge the gap in your ever-changing talent needs." This has always been good advice, and now more than ever it's critical to your success.

How Outsourcing Puts You Ahead of the Game

Nearshore and offshore outsourcing are now recognized as sound strategies for driving growth and agility, by giving companies access to deep and highly skilled talent pools. The fact that it all costs less is a bonus, but the real value comes from having the best people on your team.

This kind of borderless, employee-statusless management model (workers can be contractors, part-time employees, or full-time employees) frees businesses up to bring in people who can drive innovation with new ideas and approaches, develop game-changing products faster, and greatly enhance the customer experience.

The demand for top-level skills, which are often incredibly hard to find locally, becomes much easier to meet when borders are no longer an issue. Need to get a team of 30 senior data engineers up and running immediately? No problem. Hoping to meet diversity requirements for female developers? Consider it done. Does your project require someone with expert knowledge of an emerging technology that no one in-house has any experience with? You might find that person somewhere you may never have looked before.

Today, you can hire quality remote technology talent from more than 40 countries, which collectively represent about 40% of the world's population. Later in the book, we'll talk about how to find the specific, top-level people and partners who fully understand Western businesses and are world-class innovators in their fields, but the point of our discussion right now is to illustrate that embracing remote work—internationally—will greatly expand your available talent pool.

In the new remote management paradigm, worker value is measured by the outcomes they deliver, not by how much time they spend behind a desk. Employees know this just as well as employers do, and they're reevaluating their lifestyles to fit the new reality. Andrea O'Sullivan, director of the Center for Technology and Innovation at the James Madison Institute, a think tank in Tallahassee, Florida, told Reason.com that young computer science grads are "no longer...forced to pay several thousand dollars a month to have the privilege to live in a shoebox and ride company buses into luxurious campuses just to sit in front of a computer."

Like I said before, the biggest challenges for managers of remote teams are related to building camaraderie and fostering collaboration, which occurs less naturally when people are geographically distributed. This will only get easier over time, as digital collaboration tools improve, as targeted travel becomes a greater possibility thanks to overall cost savings, and as firms experiment with hybrid work environments and start to document best practices.

Managers of remote teams can also do lots of things to help individual team members feel appreciated and deepen their commitment to the larger group. Some companies have been offering perks to their remote workers, such as monthly wellness stipends and free lunches delivered to their homes. I know of managers who send out team T-shirts, deliver bottles of spirits for team happy hours via Zoom, and give cash bonuses for exceptional work. Personal touches like these make an impact: They are long remembered and can be powerful tools for creating team synergy and individual effectiveness.

Another important responsibility of remote team managers is to keep the lines of communication among team members wide open. Rather than just responding to questions or concerns as they arise, the best managers are proactive. They check in with each team member on a regular basis and set up office hours when their virtual doors are open to everyone. When people know that their voices will be heard, they generally have a greater sense of belonging.

The wholesale transition to the new normal of remote working has set the stage for a greater acceptance of nearshore and offshore outsourcing. As experts with decades of experience in what makes remote work most effective, quality outsourcing firms have already mastered the capacity, stability, and compliance requirements for dispersed work practices, making it much easier for more companies to embrace outsourcing as a strategy.

Outsourcing Success Story: Remote Working Before It Was Cool

Three years before the pandemic, Matt Cesarz found that his ability to recruit full-time talent couldn't keep up with his need to expand his software engineering team. As Vice President of Software Engineering for Plano, Texas-based Optimal Blue, the leading provider of secondary marketing solutions and data services for the mortgage industry, Matt decided to add a dozen full-stack Microsoft developers to his team via outsourcing.

"Finding that number of people in our tight turnaround time was daunting," he says. "Looking outside the U.S. for the kind of staffing growth that I needed was one of my objectives."

Working with our team at Accelerance, Matt increased his team by 20% within two months, and the remote-sourcing model shielded Optimal Blue's software team from two major business challenges in 2020—the pandemic and the tech talent shortage.

"We built a powerful staff augmentation model that's been serving us well for more than six years," he says. "We're not looking back."

By recruiting and managing talent in Latin America, Matt has access to a ready pool of skilled, affordable developers in time zone alignment with his U.S. operations. Thanks to English proficiency, strong communication skills, and a solid cultural fit, the Latin American team members integrate seamlessly with Matt's in-house team.

GUEST EXPERT SPOTLIGHT

PATRICK MEE

Patrick Mee is currently Executive Vice President of Engineering at NextRoll. In addition to being responsible for growing teams and how they work across two business units, he's also the executive sponsor for NextRoll's DEI committee and women's employee resource group.

Give Freedom and Inspect Frequently

Remote working works best in a no-blame culture with no second-class citizens.

Unless you treat your remote and local teams equally, you'll never develop the kind of trust and collaboration you need to succeed. It's quite simple, really: build all your processes and culture and everything else the same for your remote people as you do for your local people.

Treating a local team special gives you twice as much work to do as a manager, and that's hard. Instead, do away with first- and second-class citizens and manage everyone the same way—as one team.

Put everyone through the same rituals, like a virtual onboarding process. If you hire hundreds of people like we do, it's a waste of time to run new training classes every week. And stop using words like "contractor" and "full-time." Those are financial arrangements with your HR department: As far as you're concerned, everyone on your team is an engineer.

I've been working with globally distributed teams like this for a long time, since 2008. When COVID hit, people from other departments in the company I was at came to me for advice, sharing concerns about how they'd know if remote people were working when they couldn't see them at their desks.

"If that's how you manage people you've already got a problem," I told them. "When you create a culture where team members can be effective you get more visibility into what's going on."

This was the paradigm shift I've been fighting for for many years. At one company I joined, there was no remote work and the CEO and other executives didn't want to take the risk. So I introduced them to three engineers who had previously worked for me in a remote capacity. They were all Americans, and some of the best engineers you'd ever want to work with. They had a great conversation with the leadership team, and after they left the CEO said to me, "We need to hire those guys."

"You know they're remote," I replied.

"I don't care. We need to hire them," said the CEO.

"Great," I said. "And I have a lot more where they came from!"

Once people got comfortable with the remote model, it was easy to scale with people from other countries. I never look for outsourced talent because of the money, it's always based on the need to scale the team. I'm never trying to get rid of a U.S. engineer so I can hire two in South America, but I often tell managers they can wait six to nine months to hire a local person or get two people outside the market up and running in two months. The deliverables never change, so the choice becomes clear pretty quickly.

While scalability is always the top priority for creating blended teams, we also benefit from diversity. Having people with different viewpoints can challenge the status quo and that's something I always want to do. Plus, giving people a chance to work for a dynamic, Silicon Valley-based technology company can be incredibly motivating, especially when the opportunities they usually get are from banks or insurance companies that are years behind the latest technologies. Because our outsourced people are usually really excited to be on my teams, they tend to stay with us a long time and refer us to other great people.

We have remote people who've been with us longer than some of our local people, and if I didn't treat them right it would mean constant turnover and retraining. If you burn people out in six or nine months you have to replace them, and that constant grind just isn't efficient.

The better way is to create a culture where everyone is respected, engaged, cared for, and motivated. When I got into management I knew I didn't want to manage people like I had been managed before, and that's when I discovered some of the exciting tenets of Agile, such as pushing responsibility to the people doing the work, respecting their skills, and respecting their personal lives.

Agile provided a perfect roadmap for me as a manager. I'm not a top-down alpha who needs to be the biggest person in the room. My style is the leader follower or servant leader, and I do what I do because I want engineers to remember why they wanted to become engineers. If you can clear the B.S. out of people's lives, give them clear goals, and make them feel empowered, you get motivated people and motivated teams.

On a tactical level, what's worked best for me is to break work down into small chunks, iterate frequently, shorten the feedback loop, make adjustments, and keep doing it. My innovation to the Agile way of working is to have all my teams—local, nearshore, or blended—run one-week sprints because two weeks is too long for us. It's amazing what you can accomplish in a year when you have 52 chances to get feedback, think about what you're doing, and make it better.

My philosophy is to give freedom to team members and inspect frequently. We give people a goal and they get a week to figure it out. And at the end of the week, we do a retrospective of what we learn. And if someone made a mistake, well, we learned something and we learned it fast. I don't get pissed off about mistakes, but I do get pissed off when I see the same mistakes again and again. I half-jokingly tell people that I want them to make more interesting mistakes, because then we're really pushing things. I want people to take risks, because if you make mistakes and learn from them you become a better engineer.

We have an engineering all-hands every six weeks, and when I bring up a production issue it's usually to say how impressed I was with how quickly people identified it, resolved it, and learned from it. That's the positive reinforcement of what I call a no-blame culture. If anyone makes a mistake, the expectation is that they'll put their hand up, own it, and write a postmortem so we can all learn from the experience.

Another recommendation I'd like to share is to avoid micromanaging details and empower your teams to work in a way that suits them best. Let them come up with their schedules because they know what they're doing. Trust them: You don't have to worry about the details if you're liking the outcome.

I always try to make this easier for people by making sure there's at least some time zone overlap between in-house and outsourced team members. The reason I've always avoided India and Eastern Europe has nothing to do with the people and everything to do with how the time zone difference forces this evil thing called a handoff.

When you hand off work to somebody and they have to carry it forward while you're in bed, things rarely end up well. They never quite get things exactly right, so you end up writing completely detailed specs which makes them feel demoralized. It's a time consuming, frustrating, and inefficient process.

With freedom and flexibility, engineering teams are remarkably good about working things out themselves. Most people will start their shifts based on where the center of gravity is when it comes to time zones, overlapping with people in other time zones as needed to get a contextual understanding of the work they'll be doing after the other side ends its day. Engineers use their common time to do a mind meld on the problems at hand.

When you manage remote and local resources in these ways, anyone who's not a good fit will bubble up to the surface pretty quickly, and you can spend your time optimizing the 95% of team members who are productive and trustworthy. Why slow down 95% of your people because you're worried about who isn't carrying their weight?

If you invest heavily in the interview process, you'll weed out the egomaniacs, the rude people, and those who find success by standing on other people's heads as opposed to raising them up. Make the effort up front to hire good people who want to be stimulated, motivated, and successful. And once you get them in, whether they're from San Francisco, Buenos Aires, or anywhere else, give them exciting and interesting work and, most importantly, trust them.

"I can do things you cannot, you can do things I cannot; together we can do great things."
—*Mother Teresa*

CHAPTER 3

THE EXPANDING TALENT POOL: GREAT PEOPLE ARE EVERYWHERE

I've been involved in software development outsourcing since 1999 and I've learned quite a bit as a witness to—and a participant in—its evolution. In a nutshell, the fewer restrictions companies have when it comes to accessing top software development talent, the more freedom and flexibility they have to iterate, improve, and innovate.

With fewer staffing hiccups, particularly when it comes to finding people with specialized technology skills, companies can get application updates and new products to market much faster. Productivity skyrockets, and growth becomes more sustainable.

Firms have been perfecting the distributed team model that outsourcing relies on since the days when manufacturing companies started hiring outside firms to manage non-essential processes in a quest for efficiency.

Despite incredible results right from the start, outsourcing wasn't an easy sell for many businesses. Concerns over control, quality, customer pushback, and employee resistance are among the common objections raised over the practice of hiring talent outside the United States.

What's great about these objections is that they've given companies and their outsourcing partners a roadmap for improvement. Contracts have been refined to ensure greater quality control, most typically through the addition of enforceable service level agreements. Best practices for communication, oversight, and governance have been worked out over time. And worker concerns have been addressed through education, training, and even funds—generated from outsourcing savings—set aside to help any affected employees transition to new roles.

In point of fact, however, nearshoring and offshoring software development have had very little impact on unemployment rates and wage growth over the past several decades. Despite huge amounts of work going to countries like India, the Philippines, Vietnam, Argentina, and others, there are more people working in technology in the U.S. than ever before, and there are still more than one million unfilled IT jobs here.

When layoffs occur, as they do regularly, they're typically due to predictable cycles that affect markets worldwide. When companies in the U.S. are laying off technology workers, most of the outsourcing partners we have relationships with are doing the same, and everyone waits as patiently as they can for the next boom cycle to come along.

If you think about the historic trajectory of the technology sector, whole new categories of work have been created and new disciplines have emerged. We expect this to continue, which is why governments and business leaders around the globe are investing heavily in technology education and enterprise. If you had said 30 years ago that Vietnam would become a major technology center no one would have believed you, but the growth in that market—and others—has been incredibly impressive.

Skills Access as a Strategic Imperative

As companies have strived to increase profits and right-size according to changing market conditions over the years, outsourcing has grown from a tactical advantage for a small number of companies to a strategic imperative for most businesses in our global economy. Soon after companies experimented with distributed manufacturing teams, it became clear that the model could be applied successfully even to more critical functions, such as payroll services, auditing, customer service, and other business processes.

Back when Accelerance was founded, IT leaders were most interested in outsourcing for what were termed "non-core" or "back-office" functions, but today we're helping clients develop innovative products, execute large-scale enterprise transformation initiatives, and take advantage of high-growth opportunities that contribute to their long-term corporate goals and solidify their competitive advantage.

The relentless pace of technology has promoted multinational management to the strategic level. Because out-innovating rivals is where all the action is, companies use global teams to drive initiatives that improve data analytics, accelerate go-to-market deadlines, and personalize customer experiences. At Accelerance we're besieged by clients who want to quickly ramp up their innovation competencies, because they know that the time to get ahead or get left behind is always now.

The tipping point for outsourcing as a strategy came in about 2016, when global consultancy Deloitte elevated the status of what it called "disruptive outsourcing."

"The focus [for outsourcing] has shifted from traditional work transfer to upfront transformation and automation," asserted Deloitte's landmark global outsourcing study that year. "Organizations are recognizing that disruptive solutions can revolutionize the way they do business, and that 'buying' capabilities in the marketplace is generally faster and more scalable than developing capabilities internally."

Many restaurateurs and retailers learned this lesson during the rapid pivot to contactless pickups and payments in the early days of the pandemic. While mobile ordering was slowly gaining traction prior to 2020, the COVID-19 disruption collapsed the adoption curve from several years to just weeks for many businesses. Any retailer that was outsourcing software development prior to the pandemic leaned in hard to get their partners on the contactless ordering case as fast as possible. We all learned what could be accomplished in a short time when our survival was on the line, and now we want to operate at warp speed every day.

Finding talented people who can successfully implement the latest and greatest technologies and solutions is critical for success today and sustained growth over time. Across every industry, new players are eroding market share from established companies through advanced technological prowess. These disruptors are often leapfrogging competitors by leveraging the capabilities and experience of outsourcing partners who can hit the ground running right away.

As a driver of growth and agility, the multinational management model is focused on quickly securing and leveraging capabilities in emerging technologies—at the lowest cost possible—to make the next generational leap. Using distributed teams to develop software provides a powerful jump start to companies looking to ramp up innovation. It facilitates access to the most leading-edge capabilities available and, as a bonus, is more scalable and cost-effective than an internal build could ever be.

"Outsourcing can provide access to technologies that an organization does not have the skills or resources to develop on its own," declared KPMG in 2018, in a report about intelligent automation. "Successful future outsourcing models will make greater use of advanced technologies... and differentiate themselves more on *how* services are delivered rather than *what* is delivered."

Outsourcing Success Story: Fintech Innovation

One U.S. financial services client of ours collaborated with two offshore partners to develop a suite of sophisticated productivity tools, based on an AI-powered knowledge base. By syncing multiple complex systems via robotic process automation (RPA), the company can now approve credit and generate loan documentation online.

In a separate project, the client modernized its loan origination software and moved it to the cloud, proving that distributed teams can help re-engineer the way organizations operate and make them increasingly agile, effective, and efficient.

The Risks of Not Outsourcing

If you limit the pool of talent and technologies you can draw from, you may not be able to find the capabilities you need. Or, if you do find them, you may have to wait months for availability or pay through the nose for more immediate access.

The more you delay your projects, the more vulnerable you are to economic stagnation, falling profitability, and a lack of innovation. And, if you blow your budgets to get the capabilities you need, your great new product may take much longer to generate a profit.

You'll have to consider whether your business has the time and resources to train people internally or hire full-time employees with the skills you need, or whether it makes more sense to source these skills elsewhere on an as-needed basis.

Some skills are so specialized that they're virtually impossible to learn in a reasonable timeframe, and trying to squeeze too much out of your existing employees isn't good for you and it's not good for them. Even the best people have limits, and your in-house staff may not be able to complete all the necessary tasks demanded by a new project at the level of quality you deserve.

Current Trends in Technology Outsourcing

To benefit fully from software development outsourcing, it's important to understand the latest trends that are shaping the industry and making multinational management increasingly relevant as a strategic business model. My company regularly analyzes the high-impact waves that motivate businesses to embrace distributed teamwork, and here are some key considerations you should be thinking about as you begin your multinational management journey.

Cost and Right-Sizing Agility

In the U.S., the going rate for a contracted software engineer is about $125 per hour, while a senior data engineering role commands between $250 and $300 per hour. For the same high standard of skills, the equivalent base rate for a senior offshore engineer at a reputable software development provider is around $50 per hour, and you'll only pay $25 more per hour for a senior-level data engineer.

Benefits of Distributed Teams

- 40% to 70% reduction in development costs
- Rapid headcount adjustment

- Easier access to specialized skills
- Ability to scale back some projects and accelerate others
- Ability to drive ongoing digital transformation efforts

Developer Shortage Paradox

Tech-led companies have long been scrambling to find qualified software developers to build applications, undertake migrations, and implement new technologies. At least half of CIOs report that the lack of skilled talent makes it difficult for their companies to grow and compete.

It's no surprise that recruiting and retaining developers with the right skills are among IT's top business challenges. And poor retention isn't helping: Only 29% of IT workers are highly intent on staying with their current employers. Outsourcing stands as a tested and proven answer to talent shortages, letting you tap into the skills you urgently need on flexible terms.

Benefits of Distributed Teams

- Talent pool expansion
- Turnover burden assumed by partners
- Elimination of recruitment expenses
- Specialized skills on demand

Hyperspecialized Tech Skills

Tech talent shortages often hit hardest in highly specialized development roles, involving dynamic, fast evolving technologies such as security, cloud computing, and artificial intelligence. Since it's costly and time-consuming to build these skills in-house, software development outsourcing is becoming an increasingly popular solution for IT leaders.

Benefits of Distributed Teams

- Domain expertise in an instant
- Access to world-class talent
- High quality at a lower cost

Hybrid Team Validation

Increasing capacity through outsourcing can be achieved by hiring full teams that operate on their own, or by blending outsourced talent with members of your in-house team. We've found that most clients benefit more from a hybrid model that includes in-house and outsourced team members.

Benefits of Distributed Teams

- Fresh thinking and perspectives through team interactions
- Greater accountability
- Greater access to talent

Cybersecurity Sourcing Crisis

While cyberattacks are intensifying, cybersecurity talent is increasingly hard to find. In 2022, Cyberseek reported that unfilled cybersecurity jobs hit a record 465,000 (nearly half of total cyber positions) in the United States.

The cybersecurity workforce gap has grown more than twice as much as the workforce, according to the 2022 (ISC)^2 Cybersecurity Workforce Study. And because the gap keeps widening, more and more organizations are vulnerable to an avalanche of ransomware, phishing, cloud attacks, IoT breaches, and other threats.

By embracing multinational management, organizations gain the peace of mind that comes from having lock-tight security capabilities. Distributed teams can handle all aspects of cybersecurity, such as conducting a comprehensive risk assessment for diagnosing vulnerabilities and implementing a remediation plan to close identified gaps.

Benefits of Distributed Teams

- Ability to fill skills gaps in cyber-defense staffing
- On-demand access to dedicated security specialists
- Lower costs for experienced, credentialed resources
- Compliance with the latest security standards and best practices

Multi-Partner Sourcing

Gone are the days of favoring a single partner for all your development needs. Savvy IT leaders are looking to spread their partner portfolios globally to mitigate against future risks that can upend businesses overnight.

With most of our clients at Accelerance, we're witnessing the rise of what we call multi-partner sourcing. As cost pressures mount and U.S. businesses cut budgets, multi-shoring is an attractive way to mitigate risk versus putting all your eggs in one basket.

Benefits of Distributed Teams

- Business resilience
- Better leverage
- Unique opportunities for partner collaboration

When Should You Outsource?

Managing distributed teams makes sense when outsourcing can bring more to your business than your internal teams can, from superior results and greater innovation to a higher level of quality and professional development.

I always encourage people to practice managing multinational teams on projects where the stakes aren't too high. For your first forays into outsourcing, choose standard operations that can be easily handled by distributed talent, and find a partner with a proven track record in the kind of work you're looking for.

Once you have a few projects under your belt, become more comfortable managing people across time zones and cultures, and build strong relationships with partners who share your values and understand your objectives, then you can up the ante and outsource higher impact projects.

With a little multinational management experience, the sky's the limit for leveraging expert resources to enhance your existing software applications and develop innovative new products. Here are just some of the scenarios where outsourcing makes a lot of sense:

Data Management Operations

Data is an essential driver for any business but loading it into your systems can be extremely slow and time-consuming, especially if it's not already in a digital format. The process of data cleansing, organization, and ingestion can be readily outsourced for a fraction of the cost domestically.

Implementing Technical Advancements

It's a mistake to avoid potential opportunities because you don't have the expertise in-house. Using outsourced teams that are already up to speed on a new technology can help you keep up with, or pull ahead of, your competitors.

New Products

It's a common belief that generating new ideas is best handled in-house, but this isn't always the case. Instead of spending countless hours agonizing over a wireframe or fuzzy front end that isn't functional, it might make more sense to give some basic concepts to an experienced remote team and see what they come up with for prototyping or building a proof of concept.

Product Upgrades/Enhancements

Instead of redirecting in-house teams for small amounts of development, which can be time-consuming, it may make sense to send some of the work offshore.

Maintenance and Support Activities

Instead of burdening your existing team of in-house developers with the task of supporting and maintaining software, consider saving money and freeing up your team by outsourcing some or all of that work. You'll likely be able to keep more of your in-house team members longer if you give them new challenges and opportunities, instead of forcing them to perform mundane activities.

Temporary Staff Augmentation

Perhaps you've already got a solid team working well in-house, but you're trying to squeeze too much out of them to achieve pressing business priorities. Evidence has shown that overworked employees tend to produce lower-quality results, so a better approach is to use nearshore or offshore developers as needed to share the load. Many outsourcing providers are adept at providing additional scrum teams, or resources that can be added to existing scrum teams, wherever the need is greatest.

Cutting Burn Rate

Budgets often end up being burned through far faster than initially intended. Instead of having to go back to the corporate board or investors for another infusion of cash (which you may or may not receive), you can reduce expenses during your development periods through outsourcing.

Good Management Is Your Key to Effective Outsourcing

Having the skills in place to accomplish great things is only part of the puzzle of working with multinational teams. The other is effective management. According to KPMG, "effort and expertise are needed to address security and cyber risks, changing regulations, organizational resistance, skill gaps, and to help flatten fragmented processes" for outsourcing to pay off. In other words, you need good managers.

Former ISG partner John Keppel sounded a similar warning while he was president of the global technology research and advisory firm. "The unprecedented change brought about by ARC (automation, robotics, and cloud) and technology innovation is creating substantial opportunity but also substantial risk," he told *Nearshore Americas*, a business and technology news journal. "Clarity of leadership and strategy will be required to navigate these turbulent waters."

Outsourcing Success Story: Epiq Systems

Epiq is a worldwide provider of legal and business services for law firms, corporations, financial institutions, and government agencies. The company takes on large-scale, complex tasks for corporate counsel, law firms, and business professionals, using an award-winning technology platform that streamlines the administration of matters related to business operations, class action/mass tort, court reporting, eDiscovery, regulatory compliance, and restructuring and bankruptcy.

IT executives were challenged by leadership to increase their software product output without impacting cost, so they sought to create a hybrid insourced and outsourced development organization that could easily be ramped up over time, efficiently and cost-effectively.

With an internal team of 120 developers and a 2-to-1 developer-to-QA ratio, Epiq's IT team knew they needed more developers to handle the increasing workload and optimize current practices. They felt that adding in scalable, outsourced resources to their existing model would create the flexible team they needed.

After assessing Epiq's needs against capabilities, we recommended several nearshore outsourcing partner options and guided the restructuring of their development function through a team they chose in Argentina. The team was set up so it could easily expand from 10 to 100 developers as needed, with the capacity to run up to 12 scrum projects at any given time.

We also spent a lot of time with Epiq's in-house team to help them get comfortable working with developers in another country. Honestly, most of the U.S.-based team was excited about the idea, and grateful to have extra resources available to share the workload.

I know that our clients have been developing more ambitious plans as they've become better managers of distributed teams. They're describing what they want out of their next-level outsourcing arrangements in highly strategic terms because they've experienced the value of a borderless, employee-statusless business model firsthand.

They know they can put a significant piece of work in the hands of others without surrendering control. In fact, they understand that their direct involvement is critical when it comes to keeping projects on track. Even when our clients decide to delegate most management duties to a third party, they still need to keep communication lines open, monitor progress, respond to any issues that arise, and provide continued guidance as needed.

Setting Yourself Up for Success

If you've never outsourced before, you'll likely be making several changes to your operating model that include a structured approach to onboarding new team members and partners and getting more sophisticated about project management.

We've seen significant, tangible benefits accrue to our own clients when multinational management is done well and for the right reasons. Here are just a few of the reasons why it's so important to learn how to manage distributed teams effectively:

- An outsourcing partner can help you obtain and scale the hard-to-find (and often expensive) specialized skills required for breakthrough digital solutions.
- A dedicated development team—specifically built for a strategic initiative—can work with greater focus than a multi-tasking, over-stretched internal development department.

- An engineering team, curated and configured to your specific needs and vision from world-class talent in different locations, can offer the perfect balance of quality, creativity, and experience with leading-edge products and technologies.

Avoiding Project Pitfalls

All projects, especially those being worked on by distributed teams, need good direction and follow-through. Here are some of the common pitfalls that can easily be avoided with the right leadership mindset:

- **Lack of focus.** Step back and ask, "Why are we doing this?" Be clear on the specific outcomes you want to achieve.
- **Lack of vision.** Some software development companies will ask how many coders you need; others will give you ideas you never thought possible. Ironically, there's usually not much difference in cost between these two options.
- **Lack of ambition.** Today, it's possible to create something that would have been inconceivable just a few years ago. True innovators know what's around the next corner.
- **User experience disconnect.** Flawed design or poor implementation can be fatal—a great product won't gain traction with customers if it's difficult to use.
- **Cost obsession.** New technology solutions can give a long-term return on investment that may not immediately impact your bottom line.
- **Lack of governance.** This is one of the most critical factors in mitigating risk. Governing innovation projects can be challenging if management doesn't understand what it takes to effect change.

Because software product cycle times are getting shorter and shorter, working with distributed teams can give your organization rapid access to technology and process experts. This is critical for growth and profitability, especially when project scope or time constraints delay the ability to establish these competencies in-house.

A borderless and employee-statusless management model lets you meet temporary software product development needs without making long-term commitments. It can also be used to pursue multiple projects simultaneously with limited staff, thus generating a richer, more robust product pipeline.

With multinational management gaining strategic importance, partner engagements and relationships have become more demanding and complex. It's more important than ever for businesses to have leaders who know how to find the best partners and manage them effectively. By the time you finish reading this book, you'll have a better understanding of the partner vetting process and the day-to-day skills you need to keep ever more strategic development and engineering initiatives on track toward successful completion.

In the next chapter, we'll talk about improving your multinational management readiness so you can hit the ground running when you make the decision to bring in talent from other countries.

One key component we'll delve into is creating a governance framework that establishes management layers, highlights best practices, and specifies remediation actions if something goes wrong. This framework will become a valuable roadmap for your future, so one project can roll right into another without having to start from scratch.

GUEST EXPERT SPOTLIGHT

PETE PANAGAKIS

A transformational leader who helps companies leverage technology to optimize business performance, Pete Panagakis has led global organizations across diverse industries, including financial services, tax, legal, energy, and telecommunications. He is currently the Chief Technology Officer at i3 Verticals.

For Effective Outsourcing, Play to Your Weaknesses

Using external teams is a great way to fill the technology gaps that are slowing you down.

The ability to tap into a global workforce gives you incredible opportunities to expand and extend your in-house team. With so many people working remotely now, it's really gotten to the point where we don't know where anybody exists—and that's okay.

If you're new to outsourcing, the goal is to blend your in-house and outsourced talent as quickly as possible. You're testing code, they're testing code, and everything starts to gel when you realize you're all working toward the same goals.

I've had partner relationships get off to a rocky start, but all it usually takes is a little clear communication to get everybody speaking the same language and creating the kind of bonds and experiences that strengthen relationships. One group I hired initially just expected to throw things over the fence, without realizing they had to be part of the daily sprints and other Agile ceremonies we were conducting. The first week was rough, but once they realized they needed to be included—and that their feedback was appreciated—the barriers broke down and everything worked out great. The second week was as different as night and day, and as one incremental success led to another the team became cohesive and was really able to pick up the velocity.

I've been outsourcing for more than 20 years, and every time I do it I learn something new. Over the years, I've found that it's always best to have as many senior and mid-senior people on your outsourced team as possible. You can add junior people later, but you're more likely to hit the ground running and achieve quick wins with people who have experience.

You also want to make sure you have a great delivery manager, because that's the day-to-day contact you'll rely on to get you all the resources you need. In our current engagement, we hired the partner we're working with because the delivery manager made such a great impression on us. He completely understood what we were doing and knew exactly what we were looking for.

In addition to having senior-level people on your team and an all-star delivery manager, one of the most important things I've learned about outsourcing is that you've got to know your strengths and weaknesses and outsource your weaknesses. One company I worked for had some quality issues, so we found a partner that was strong in quality assurance and understood it to a T. We didn't have that strength, and it's very expensive to build in-house, so I thought if we could find a partner better than us in that area they could raise the bar for the whole team.

And that's exactly what our partner did in that situation. They helped us build test cases. They helped us work through regression testing.

They basically brought us all the functions that a formal quality assurance department or team should have. They even offered to train up our existing people: Some of them really stepped up to match the level of our partner, while others decided to pursue other opportunities.

I could have hired an in-house quality manager, and we could have slowly replaced or trained some of our existing resources ourselves, but it would've taken at least six months to a year before we'd even start to get decent results. By augmenting a weak part of our team with outsourced experts, we drastically improved our QA program within three months.

Every situation is different, so you have to go in with your eyes wide open before you make any decisions or assumptions. The more you take advantage of outsourcing, the more use cases and workloads you'll find for it if you think creatively, look for new opportunities, and explore new ways of leveraging resources. It's all about opening the enterprise imagination for what can be done.

Very recently, I was literally shocked to find out that we could outsource some of our important governance, risk, and compliance (GRC) work. It literally blew me away to find out that one of our offshore partners had this kind of experience, and it's something we're considering very seriously. We're envisioning a leadership team in the U.S. working directly with auditors, while an offshore team does the heavy lifting of managing and maintaining the necessary controls.

Most recently, I hired an outsourcing partner that's helping my current company even out our technological maturity. Our organization was built on acquisitions, so we have different technologies all over the place and needed a partner with expertise in many areas. They're based in Brazil, but they have offices all over the globe and provide a wide range of skills and talent. It's been working out great, and they've been extremely helpful with some of our key cloud initiatives.

Whether you need help with the cloud, GRC, cybersecurity, help desk, scaling a machine learning model, or just good old fashioned software development, the possibilities for outsourcing are tremendous in the times we're living in. And because we're drastically moving toward a global market with pockets of talent everywhere, leveraging resources around the world just makes sense.

"No one can whistle a symphony. It takes a whole orchestra to play it."
—H.E. Luccock

CHAPTER 4

IS YOUR BUSINESS READY FOR MULTINATIONAL MANAGEMENT?

So how do you know if your business is ready to operate successfully in the new globally distributed reality? You can be 100% committed to multinational management and outsourcing, but without understanding your strengths and weaknesses—and setting an accurate baseline for your readiness to manage global teams—you may be setting yourself up to fail.

You must be willing to address organizational issues and capability gaps before you initiate a multinational management engagement. If you aren't, software outsourcing can turn into a disaster of blown budgets and delays—which is what you want to AVOID by outsourcing in the first place.

In this chapter, I'll help you identify the capabilities and resources you already have. I'll also help you fill in any gaps that might prohibit you from successfully leveraging and managing outsourcing partnerships and multinational teams. Most projects fail because of internal weaknesses;

dealing with these issues upfront can significantly impact your ability to master the new distributed business environment.

Baseline: A Proven Way to Lower Your Risk

Baseline is a system we use to get a full picture of your current processes, leadership structure, skill sets, technologies, culture, and business problems to determine whether you should pursue outsourcing. If the answer is yes, Baseline helps identify red flags and determines what you need to do right away to improve your readiness. Throughout the process, you'll gain valuable insights about yourself, your business, and how software outsourcing can help you achieve your goals.

After more than 20 years of helping clients large and small find and work successfully with outsourcing partners, often in the wake of massive failures, my team and I have seen it all when it comes to the factors that can doom an outsourcing relationship from the very start.

With Baseline, we analyze 15 critical risk factors in software development outsourcing. Because the success or failure of software outsourcing projects is predictable and manageable, you'll have a much better chance at success if you assess and mitigate these risk factors early on.

Keep in mind, however, that even if you've got most of the areas covered it's not enough—a chain is only as strong as its weakest link. So it's important to shore up your readiness in all 15 areas before you start an outsourcing engagement.

We break the 15 risk factors down into three categories—business, management, and technology—so you can understand what you need to do to ensure that your investment of time and money in a software outsourcing relationship yields the highest possible return for your company.

In our experience, how you begin will likely determine how you end. Unless you've thought through how you're going to build what it is you want to build—and who is going to be responsible for that—you're not going to have great success.

Business Risks That Can Cause Software Outsourcing to Fail

Ad hoc processes, inconsistent priorities, and poor leadership can undermine your outsourcing efforts. Be sure to consider these five factors and always strive to keep a strong tie-in between your business needs and desired outcomes.

Business Risk #1: Undefined Metrics
Key players in business and IT must be able to answer this question: "What does success look like?" A project charter or other mission statement should be tied to expected and quantified outcomes:

- Will we gain market share? (What is the revenue impact?)
- Will we improve operational efficiency? (What are the cost savings?)
- Will we increase transactional velocity? (What is the anticipated delta?)
- Will we create higher levels of customer loyalty? (How will that be calculated?)

Your business objectives should be described in measurable terms and become your North Star for navigating successful projects.

Business Risk #2: Inconsistent Priorities
Because software development is full of compromise and negotiation, priorities should be fully understood and agreed upon by the lines of business affected, the IT staff, and everyone on the project team.

Which elements (capabilities, functions, and features) of your software solution matter most? For companies using iterative development and deployment techniques (Agile sprints, for example), it's imperative to have a work program that's shaped by priorities the business areas have endorsed.

A concept often overlooked in software development, especially with iterative production releases, is the concept of a minimum viable product (MVP). Companies should be highly attuned to what end users value most, because too many software releases are met with a "so what, who cares?" type of response.

Business Risk #3: Few Executive Champions

Leaders set the tone for their teams and are ultimately the "culture keepers." If senior managers don't reinforce the importance of an initiative through words and actions, then it's foolish to presume that department stakeholders will make any kind of commitment to the project.

It's widely known that the lack of executive buy-in and sponsorship is a key reason for project failure. Executive sponsors are irreplaceable when it comes to facilitating change management, affirming goals, and resolving conflicts.

Business Risk #4: Lack of Team Engagement

Sometimes a third party is set up for failure because they aren't engaged by your company employees in appropriate ways, or business stakeholders don't put in the time or energy required to achieve success.

Be sure to consider how the people you tap for help inside your company, including subject matter experts (SMEs), will be able to commit time to the project while keeping their other commitments on track.

Business Risk #5: Partnership Relations

Your software outsourcing vendor is an extension of your internal team's capabilities. Their success is YOUR success. This is why we encourage companies to embrace the mindset of "covenant" versus "contract."

When business partners are in a covenant with each other, they both strive to achieve a common goal. In contrast, third-party vendors are simply expected to ship goods or provide services for a predetermined price. This usually doesn't work for custom software development because requirements are constantly changing, and relationships generally need to operate on a plane that goes beyond transactional.

An effective software development outsourcing partnership begins with identifying specific skills and compatible stylistic characteristics. Sometimes being compatible means that your partners are methodical, like you. Other times, it means that they're MORE methodical and systematic in their approach, to keep you honest.

Business partners need to know—and they appreciate knowing—the criteria that will determine success and the potential barriers that might prevent success. Your "win" and their "win" should be the same.

Business Risks: Questions to Consider

Are you committing the right people, processes, and resources internally to lead to overall success?

Metrics

- Are business goals and metrics clearly defined?
- How will you measure the success of the project?
- How does this project support overall organizational goals, objectives, and KPIs?

Priorities

- What features deliver the most value to the business?
- Which features are must haves vs. good to haves?
- Is there a shared understanding of priorities among internal team members?

Executive Champions

- Will the right leaders allocate the right amount of time and attention?

- Where does this project fit among executive goals, objectives, and KPIs?

Team Engagement

- Are the right team members from your organization committed to success and available to help?
- Are your internal team members committed to working with and supporting your outsourced partners?

Partner Relations

- Will you strive for a collaborative relationship over a transactional one?
- How will each organization ensure the other's success?

Outsourcing Success Story: Risk Factor Mitigation

One of our clients identified a need to mitigate risk in the areas of executive engagement, process improvement, and team communications before starting a multinational management journey. Our "quick win" recommendations included bringing in help for quality assurance and establishing an emergency team to tackle urgent items for existing customers.

Our long-term recommendations included a detailed plan for streamlining processes and increasing transparency. Conflicting priorities and requests from service delivery, support, customer success, and product were all wasting engineering resources and needed sorting out before it made sense to work with an outsourcing partner.

After months of hard work, the client began working with a right-fit partner and the first project was a home run. Since then, the client has been consistently outsourcing development work with multiple partners.

Management Risks That Can Cause Software Outsourcing to Fail

The second category of risk involves your ability to ensure that your project goals are pursued with intentionality, clarity, and healthy team dynamics.

If the people responsible for stewarding a project fail to establish a good structure and team dynamics, an otherwise viable project (good concept, clear business benefits, capable partners, solid technology) becomes a rudderless ship at sea.

One situation that exacerbates this type of risk is the growing adoption of Agile and other highly iterative development methodologies at the expense of a commitment to clear milestones and progress tracking. Don't abandon project management rigor to gain speed and nimbleness. Instead, strive to have it all.

Management Risk #1: Unrealistic Expectations

Any leader with experience in contractual relationships knows that disagreements can arise over obligations, and that the gray area of expectations and assumptions is typically where risk occurs. Reasonable parties working together can usually find a palatable compromise, but unrealistic expectations can derail a relationship.

How do unrealistic expectations bubble up to the surface? Often, we see customers take a very hard line on due dates or costs, without regard for delays caused by their own lack of involvement. It's never a good idea to presume that your outsourcing partners can make up for lost time.

Unrealistic expectations can also arise when internal team leaders assume that industry expertise is the same as company intimacy. While vertical expertise is an important thing to look for in your international partners, you must also let them in on the nuances of your company culture, organizational structure, business models, and products that can impact their effectiveness if not properly understood.

Management Risk #2: Unfocused Leadership

Sometimes the right stakeholders are assigned to a project but fail to give it the attention it requires. Will internal project leaders need some backfill or bandwidth to ensure that other business needs are addressed? Have other business priorities been properly factored into what may land on each person's plate?

Distracted project managers who fail to enforce progress against plan, ignore status reports, and avoid tracking project metrics are definitely a liability.

Management Risk #3: Unclear Milestones

In the days of the Waterfall methodology, projects proceeded in a linear fashion and "Go Live" was a single "Big Bang" event. These days, continuous deployment through methodologies like Agile means that the expected iterative milestones need to be extremely clear.

Otherwise, features can be overlooked in a long sequence of production releases. Words you never want to hear during a software development project are, "Oh, I just assumed that was part of the next release."

Management Risk #4: Lack of Team Interaction

Good communication has always been important in software development projects. In an age of iterative development and deployment, multi-geographical teams, multiple time zones, and a pace that can border on frenetic, good communication is an essential core competency of the project team.

Processes and collaborative technologies must come together in a harmonious way to ensure that the constant back-and-forth handoffs among internal and external participants are seamless and transparent.

When "walking down the hall" isn't an option, it's critical that project leaders create clear constructs for effective communication. Regular, effective status meetings are crucial, as are digital tools that allow all team members to see tasks, responsibilities, and progress at a glance.

Management Risk #5: Weak Processes

Technology can never overcome bad processes in a software development project. Your project roadmap must be fully understood, and all team members must be fluent and diligent in the methods required to bring the project over the finish line.

Management Risks: Questions to Consider

Do you have the skills, tools, and experience to run projects efficiently and effectively?

Unrealistic Expectations

- Are you initiating your project with eyes wide open?
- Are expectations understood and agreed to by all internal team members?

Unfocused Leadership

- Are the right internal people assigned to your project?
- Do they have the availability to manage it?

Unclear Milestones

- How will progress be defined, measured, and understood by all stakeholders?
- How will you know if your project is on schedule (green/yellow/red)?
- Who will watch and hold the team accountable?

Lack of Team Interactions

- How will you ensure that handoffs among internal and outsourced team members don't break down?
- Have time zone issues and cultural differences been identified and addressed?

- How effective is your communication?
- Will each meeting produce specific action items?

Weak Processes

- Are your roadmap and methodologies laid out and understood?
- Is your software development lifecycle established and accepted by all stakeholders?
- What tools will you use to measure progress?

Technology Risks That Can Cause Software Outsourcing to Fail

Technology risks stem from the tools, methods, and approaches controlled by your IT team.

Technology Risk #1: Inadequate Skills

It's surprising how often outsourcing partners aren't properly vetted to confirm that they have the skills and experience they need to be successful. Before contracting, make sure you review certifications, training, experience, and references.

Is industry or vertical experience part of the skill set you need? Make sure that your partner has experience developing solutions that reasonably match your business context. Each project circumstance is unique, so ask your potential partners how their experiences match up well with your situation.

Adequate skills must also be backed up by sufficient bench strength. It's important that the success of your project doesn't hinge on a single, niche talent. The best outsourcing partners can demonstrate a culture of continuous education, cross-training, and recertification.

Technology Risk #2: Undefined Operations

A driving force behind the emergence of Development Operations (DevOps) was the gap between applications and operations, which must work well together during development and deployment. Adding outsourced team members into the mix is an effective way of getting work done, but it also adds complexity.

Who's responsible for hosting? How will the software be certified for the intended target platform and who will do it? Will pre-production and production be managed by the same group? It's imperative that the architecture, release levels, and other aspects of the "dev," "test," and "production" environments are equivalent.

Make sure both you and your outsourcing partner understand each party's responsibilities from start to finish.

Technology Risk #3: Ineffective Design

Because form follows function, product design must drive a solution that achieves core business goals. You want to ensure that your beautiful new web application will launch and function properly on mobile devices. You also want to make sure that users receive the best possible experience, so they don't leave early or abandon their purchases.

Technology Risk #4: Lack of Quality Assurance

The speed of Agile development, along with the opportunity to deploy code to production more rapidly, may create a temptation to overlook or minimize good quality assurance (QA). Moreover, a software outsourcer may not understand what QA steps are expected or demanded by policy or regulation.

Are QA procedures in place and understood by both parties? Are they robust enough? Are the standards for the software clearly understood? It's very important to establish expectations for quality assurance in advance.

Technology Risk #5: Technical Debt

I often see companies with a large backlog of serious technology issues. Applications lack competitive functionality or require critical upgrades just to stay viable. If your software isn't currently up to date, you'll likely have to expand your development budget and build in extra time to get things done.

Examine your company's technical backlog carefully. How bad is it? Is there a process in place to remedy the debt? Will you have to do that first before you start a new software development initiative?

Technology Risks: Questions to Consider

Will the team you've assembled deliver the desired results?

Inadequate Skills

- Do your outsourced team members have the right technical experience?
- Are they adequately trained?
- How do you know?

Undefined Operations

- Do both sides understand who will handle hosting and testing?
- How will the software be optimized for the intended platform?

Ineffective Design

- Is there a good fit between your business requirements and the user experience?

Lack of Quality Assurance

- Are QA procedures in place and understood by both sides?
- Are your QA procedures robust enough to comply with any regulatory requirements?
- Are software standards clearly understood?

Technical Debt

- What is your threshold for acceptable technical debt?
- Is there a process in place to pay it off?
- How will you ensure the ongoing maintenance of your software?

Key Considerations for Determining Your Readiness

To get the most out of our Baseline process—and any engagements that require the management of multinational teams—you'll want to examine your organization through the lens of the following five characteristics:

1. **Risk Tolerance**
   If your company's culture is conservative, you may not want to jump into high impact or complex projects before you get comfortable managing distributed teams.

2. **Process Integrity**
   If your processes are unpredictable, poorly controlled, and reactive, outsourcing engagements can expose your company to unnecessary risk.

3. **Experience Level**
   It's important to include at least some senior people on projects that use distributed teams. If no one at your company is advanced in their level of experience or capabilities, then it might be worth hiring a consultant to help manage the first few projects.

   If people in your company are new to management roles, keep an eye out for those you'd describe as good systems thinkers. These people are very likely to catch on quickly and become valuable assets when it comes to getting things done.

4. **Outsourcing Resistance**
   As I've mentioned before, outsourcing has gotten a bad reputation in some business circles. Be sure to listen to any internal concerns and address them with honesty and respect. You want as much buy-in for multinational management projects from as many people as possible, especially at the highest levels in your company.

   Confidence that your project will contribute to your company's overall growth and performance will go a long way toward generating enthusiasm for the multinational management model.

5. **Collaborative Nature**
Egos should always be left at the door when teams are involved, but it's even more important when people are separated by expanses of time and distance. For multinational management projects to work, extra effort must be made to share information and keep all your team members in the loop.

What Is Your Risk Capability Maturity Level?

Assessing your risk capability maturity level is another exercise you should go through before embarking on a partnership with a software outsourcing provider.

While proactive risk mitigation should be the goal of any effective organization, not all companies are currently at that level. Use the descriptions below to determine what level your organization is at today and work to achieve something higher if you can. If you're not at Level 3, you may want to delay any outsourcing commitments until you get a better handle on risk management and remove organizational issues that could derail your outsourcing projects.

Risk Capability Maturity Levels

Level 1: Ad Hoc
Processes are unpredictable, poorly controlled, and reactive.

Organizations at this level have little or no data integration among business functions. Disparate systems create gaps in processes and metrics are not in place. An organization may have some high-performing areas, but for the most part management is inconsistent.

Level 2: Defined
Defined risk management capabilities are in place.

Organizations at this level recognize the need for risk management and have some tools in place to get the job done. Meeting decisions are tracked to some degree, and a project management or enterprise resource planning (ERP) system may be in use to consolidate information and generate insights. Standardization of processes and systems across the enterprise is often talked about and multiple functions may be sharing information and collaborating. Full integration may not have been achieved, but information is available to aid better decision making.

Level 3: Managed
Standardized processes are in place.

Organizations at this level take advantage of real-time information to make critical decisions. Improved communication and coordination facilitate synchronized risk management at an enterprise level, and visible performance metrics are acted upon to improve performance. While there are clear opportunities for more process integration, things are moving in the right direction.

Level 4: Integrated
Governed processes, metrics, and technology platforms for risk management are in place.

Organizations at this level have a comprehensive risk management strategy. Leadership receives regular reports and uses risk management insights to make informed decisions. Steady upgrades in capabilities are made over time and integration is happening at all levels. Key performance indicators (KPIs) act as essential decision-making tools within teams, and human error is significantly reduced because integration and automation are well underway.

Level 5: Optimized
The ultimate strategic, systemized risk management function is in place and regularly reviewed and upgraded.

Organizations at this level apply best practices and state-of-the-art technologies across all functions. Leadership understands the benefits of advanced risk management and recognizes that if they're not leveraged and utilized properly, poor performance and costly decisions may result. Leaders are looking for continuous improvement. KPIs are updated in real time and are a primary source of risk mitigation and informed decision making. Information, insights, and learnings are readily available and routinely used to help the organization progress.

Choosing Confidence-Building Projects

Any management project requires a commitment of time and money, so it's important to review your priorities and assess which projects make the most sense for adding people from other countries.

When you work with multinational teams on projects that are proven to benefit from outsourced talent, you'll gain the confidence and experience you need to add international talent to even more of your teams.

When choosing projects for software development outsourcing, ask yourself the following questions:

Which projects will provide the best return on investment?
Initiatives with a clear business benefit will generally get better buy-in and higher quality participation.

Which projects have the clearest goals and scope?
Clarity of vision is a key factor in ensuring successful outcomes.

Do any projects require new or unproven technologies?
Unfamiliar technology can be problematic if you don't have access to the right resources. On the other hand, projects that require these technologies are good candidates for outside talent who can bring in that expertise.

Does your project require integration with other systems?
Integration testing can be very time-consuming and requires a higher level of coordination.

Which projects are expected to have the longest duration?
Variables beyond your control pose a higher risk in long-running projects, such as key personnel changes, loss of momentum, and other business distractions.

Which projects are expected to require the largest number of participants?
Project complexity increases as more people get involved.

Get Your House in Order before You Place an Outsourcing Order

Most companies are unaware of the proper preparation that should take place before entering an outsourcing engagement. Tech leaders who jump straight to partner selection overlook the potential—and often all too obvious—risk factors within their organization that could derail a project that would otherwise have been a slam dunk.

While I'm certainly one of outsourcing's biggest proponents, I'm not shy about telling executives at different companies not to do it until they get critical aspects of their business culture and processes, management and leadership structures, and technological resources and thought processes figured out in advance. It's much better to wait six months or even a year and have a successful outsourcing project than it is to start now and have a catastrophic failure on your hands.

I hope this chapter gave you a better understanding of the 15 risk factors you need to consider to find success with multinational management and outsourcing. Chances are, you may only need to strengthen a handful of areas to get yourself ready for your first outsourcing engagement, but be sure to take an honest assessment of where your company is today and build your readiness before engaging with an outsourcing partner.

GUEST EXPERT SPOTLIGHT

ERIK SEVERINGHAUS

A veteran of the entrepreneurial arena, Erik Severinghouse has helped create new technology in artificial intelligence, cloud software, and other fields. He's currently the Co-Founder and Co-CEO of Bloomfilter, which is pioneering the System of Intelligence category for software development. Erik is also the author of "Scale Your Everest," a guidebook for entrepreneurs that want to build up their mental resilience. He summited the famous peak in 2018.

Taking Stupidity Out of Your Processes

How shared understanding and empathy lead to better outcomes.

The whole world has been wrestling with what the software development industry has been trying to figure out for the past 20 years: How do managers understand what's going on when they can't walk around the office anymore?

When all my developers worked in house, I could ask them what they were building. Some of them might have smelled funny and told me a bunch of words I couldn't understand, but at least I got an answer. With nearshore and offshore developers, as well as remote workers in our own countries, we risk a greater loss of control over our projects. This must be offset by a radical process evolution that focuses on mutual understanding and empathy.

Without alignment on requirements and goals, clear communication, and trust, the people doing your work are going to get confused, frustrated, and disillusioned. These conditions rarely lead to great software, but they're reaching epidemic proportions. The fact that 78% of software projects are late, over budget, or don't ship at all is a definite sign of dysfunctional business processes at work, and those are largely tied to a lack of shared understanding and empathy among different parts of an organization.

Any kid who's ever played telephone understands that information loses fidelity as it flows through different nodes. The big problem I see all over the place is that software developers have one idea of what's going on, product managers have another, and they're both completely different from what the folks in the executive suite are thinking. There's a massive disconnect around what's being built, when it's going to be ready, and how much it's going to cost.

Businesspeople yell at the programmers, wondering why they're not working harder. Meanwhile, the programmers are wondering why the requirements are changing every week, making it impossible to get anything accomplished.

When a finance executive keeps authorizing spending for more developers and the output doesn't increase, the natural assumption is that the developers are incompetent, lazy, or out to sabotage the project. Assumptions like that, in the absence of real information, erode trust and make collaboration more difficult, creating a downward spiral where everything gets worse and worse and worse.

Recently, through a company I started called Bloomfilter, I've been helping clients break down and evaluate their business processes to get a more accurate idea of what's going on. One of our clients kept missing sprint goals and deadlines, for example, and the executive team was getting upset. The organization kept hiring more developers to get things moving faster, but nothing changed.

Once we modeled the process flow, we saw that the bottleneck was occurring in QA, not development. Hiring more developers was actually exacerbating the problem! So we moved QA forward in the process and had them work with smaller chunks of code to identify and remediate issues before the production line got off kilter.

This new approach, based on a shared understanding of what was going on and empathy for the developers and businesspeople, made a huge difference. The developers began focusing on what they loved to do and their velocity increased. They were so grateful that somebody cared enough to address the stupidity in the process so they could be more effective in their jobs. Similarly, the businesspeople relaxed because things started working.

Once a team starts doing the things it says it's going to do, momentum starts taking over on both the execution side and the oversight side. The oversight team has so much more trust when the team falls into a business rhythm and acts in a predictable manner. And the execution team really starts to get engaged and have fun.

Process modeling is one way to facilitate shared understanding and empathy, and another way is to have meaningful conversations. In certain parts of the world, for example, people are uncomfortable pushing back because it feels culturally inappropriate. So if you find that your outsourcing partner is saying yes to everything but nothing gets done, you may need to find a different way of asking questions: How do you think we should handle this? What are your thoughts about this approach?

It all comes back to the idea of empathy and shared understanding. If we can create visibility into processes and communicate effectively, we can find out what's breaking and work together to make things more efficient, predictable, and functional.

Most well-meaning, well-educated people want to do well by their colleagues, customers, and various other stakeholders. We forget sometimes, especially across cultural boundaries, that the thing we all share as humans is an innate desire to do the right thing, work hard, and accomplish goals.

Once you establish the trust that comes from shared understanding and empathy, you can more easily keep your projects on track and make any adjustments you need to make along the way. Because you're building something unique and bespoke, it's really important to understand that the real value in software development comes from building the right thing, not building the wrong thing faster.

You'll know you're ready for software development outsourcing when you're willing to think about the business processes of software development in a different way. It's not about how many pull requests or lines of code a developer writes, it's about how efficiently we're capturing requirements, considering inputs, and creating great design. If those parts of the process are done exceptionally well—by team members who have a shared understanding of the project and empathy for each other—the coding almost takes care of itself. And by the time your product goes into user acceptance testing, there's no question you've done the right thing.

"Individual commitment to a group effort—that is what makes a team work, a company work, a society work, a civilization work."
—*Vince Lombardi*

CHAPTER 5

DEAL PARAMETERS: UNDERSTANDING DIFFERENT STRUCTURES

While you're getting your internal teams and business stakeholders ready for multinational management, you can also start to think about how your future outsourcing deals might be structured. In this chapter, we'll talk about different team configurations, pricing models, and service level agreements that can help you maximize the success of projects that involve multinational teams.

Each approach will deliver cost savings and other operational benefits, but you might choose one approach over another based on factors related to your specific goals, objectives, and vision. If your primary concern is short-term cost savings and staffing flexibility, your approach may be different from an organization that puts more of an emphasis on process control and intellectual property protection.

Structuring Your Outsourced Teams for Success

Companies can add outsourced human resources in several different ways, and the choices you make will have an impact on your results. There's no right or wrong here, but you should understand the options and decide what will work best for you in specific circumstances.

The Staff Augmentation—or Hybrid—Model

One of the fastest-growing team approaches is called the staff augmentation model, which is also known as the hybrid model. It involves sourcing talent from external outsourcing partners and mixing them into your existing in-house team.

Augmenting your in-house team with professionals from an outsourcing partner can help you fast-track projects, sidestep lengthy recruiting processes, and quickly adapt to changing business conditions. It can also provide the fresh perspective and innovation boost we've been talking about throughout the book.

Using this approach, you'll likely be looking for people with a wide range of skill sets. You may need people who have the same skills as your existing team members if you just need to expand capacity, you might need people with complementary skills, or you might need people with specialized skills that you just don't have in-house. Staff augmentation is fast and flexible and can be used for a range of situations, such as accelerating the development of a new business application, adding specialists to a current project, and bolstering entire programs of work.

Staff augmentation allows you to realize significant cost savings, between 30% and 70% per person. In addition to lower labor rates, you avoid many of the costs associated with hiring full-time employees, such as talent development, benefits, bonuses, and overhead.

Tech Labor Cost Savings from Staff Augmentation Outsourcing

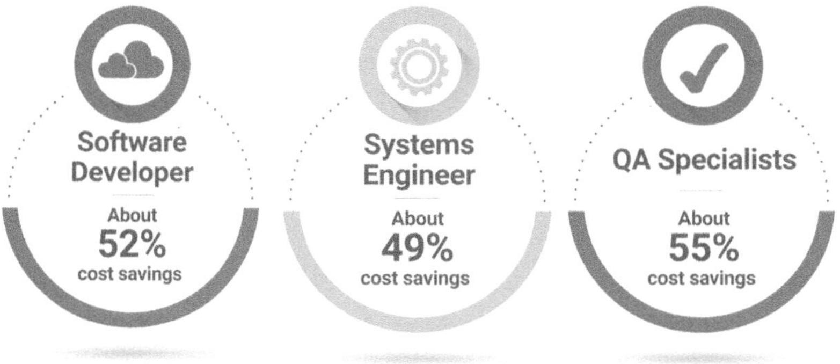

With the staff augmentation model, the day-to-day management burden is on you as you work with internal and external team members at the same time. The main reason why I wrote this book is to help you learn the multinational management best practices you need to feel comfortable with this popular outsourcing model. While you'll also need to understand the principles of multinational management with the other team models we'll be talking about, they really come into play here because the management role is very direct.

The most positive aspect of the staff augmentation model is that you maintain tight control over your entire team. The downside is that you're relying on new people who haven't lived and breathed your company culture. That's why it's so important to manage hybrid teams effectively by understanding how to facilitate collaboration and keep lines of communication open across the cultural divide (more on this in Chapter 7).

Staff augmentation has proven its worth time and time again, and organizations that use it to develop strong relationships generally fare better in volatile times.

The Project Model

Project outsourcing is slightly different from staff augmentation because it involves turning over accountability for an entire development project—or parts of an enterprise program—to an outsourcing firm. In most situations, the outsourced team remains distinct and independent, with little, if any, interaction with any of your in-house team members.

While you'll collaborate with your outsourcing partner to make sure your project stays on track, they'll be responsible for day-to-day team management and your internal people will be less involved, if at all.

This type of model is good for organizations that currently don't have any internal software development resources, already have internal resources committed to other projects, or need complete teams with specialized skills that aren't available internally. Project outsourcing is good for long-term, strategic projects with experienced partner organizations that have already done similar work for other businesses

Augmentation vs. Project Outsourcing

Considerations	Staff Augmentation	Project Outsourcing
Project Management	Covered in-house	Shared responsibility with partner
Expertise	Mainly software developers	Developers, specialists, and managers
Project Duration	Short-term, rapid-turn projects	Long-term strategic projects
Cost Levels	Varies based on expertise involved	Highly predictable per budget
TOP PRIORITY	Accessing resources	Achieving desired results

The Captive Model

A captive outsourcing model is interesting because it involves setting up a corporate-owned subsidiary in a nearshore or offshore location. While companies with the resources and local knowledge can create captive centers from scratch or purchase an existing software development company in the particular area, deals like this often follow what's known as a build-operate-transfer (BOT) approach. A vendor is hired to set up, staff, and operate a captive center for a predefined time, after which ownership is transferred to the sponsoring entity.

Beyond technical expertise, the partner firm provides a vital logistical function, knowledge of the local market (location, taxes), human resource capabilities (recruiting, training, payroll), and goodwill within the community.

Software outsourcing BOTs come in a variety of forms, generally oriented around the length of engagement and degree of involvement. One company may want their outsourcing partner to establish a new location with separate and distinct recruiting, training, and management functions, while another company may be okay if the partner builds a new team at its own, existing location. In the latter scenario, the company has greater flexibility because it can trigger the transfer as planned, or, if circumstances change, maintain the relationship as is without investing in a new facility.

Given the effort required to build, operate, and transfer a captive center, we've found that critical mass occurs at 20 or more full-time employees once the transfer goes into effect. Direct management of teams smaller than this can be difficult, as team members can feel isolated without a clear career path from a remote employer.

Most transfers in BOT deals don't occur for at least 18–24 months after the start of the relationship. This gives the outsourcing partner time to establish a stable, vibrant work culture that will benefit the sponsoring company for years to come after the transfer takes place.

Sometimes these captive subsidiaries will outsource a significant portion of non-core work (hybrid captive model) or even become an outsourcing partner for other customers (shared captive model). In the shared captive model, the subsidiary becomes a potential revenue generator for the parent company.

Outsourcing Pricing Models

When you're negotiating with a software development partner for an outsourced project, selecting the right pricing model is crucial for getting the most value from your investment. Your pricing model should have the right balance between your budget expectations, timeline, and quality goals, and an effective upfront negotiating process will help set you up for success. Pricing structure is one of the top three reasons (56%) why companies renegotiate their outsourcing contracts, according to a study by Boston Consulting Group (BCG).

While going into any engagement with a keen eye on price is important, keep in mind that just by outsourcing you'll be able to save significant amounts of money.

Fixed Pricing

Fixed price contracts can be advantageous for small projects with a clearly defined scope and a stable set of requirements, such as minor enhancements to an existing software application. For larger projects, however, fixed price models are rarely the best option. Here are some of the reasons why:

- Most fixed price contracts are padded for risk contingency: If your design specifications aren't complete, your partner will need to make many assumptions to come up with a bid.
- Most fixed price models require money up front.
- You have one chance to document everything you want designed into your software: Anything left out will have to be managed by change orders, which can be very frustrating.

- Instead of incremental design and sprints of completed work, a development team on a fixed price contract typically deploys software in larger big bang phases. This forfeits the benefits of speed and effective design made possible using an Agile development framework.

Most providers in a fixed price model will request payments as they deliver on specific project milestones. Variations and change orders can become part of the landscape if there's a change of scope or if the client causes delays: These can cause cost blowouts and should be carefully managed.

For services that can't reasonably be quantified when the contract is signed, ensure that you have provisions in place for addressing new requirements at reasonable rates. A rate card is essential so you know what you'll be paying for each distinct resource, and you should reserve the right to contract extra work on either a fixed price or time and materials basis.

Costs are generally higher using a fixed price model. Expect your software development partner to include a contingency of at least 15% for simple projects if they know you well and are comfortable working with you. And expect higher contingency rates for custom software development engagements with new partners—30% is not unusual for complex projects.

Time and Materials

This model is great for long-term projects because it allows for scope flexibility and avoids the contingency fees usually applied to fixed price projects. If you can communicate your needs and find an outsourcing partner that's good at accurately estimating projects like yours, you'll have fewer surprises at the end of the engagement.

To minimize scope creep, it's important to build effective project management teams to ensure that the work gets finished on time and on budget. You'll need to be confident that you can track project performance consistently and avoid costly delays.

Incentive-Based Pricing

Often an add-on to one of the models described above, incentive-based pricing enables extra payments—on top of the price estimated in the original contract—when the development team exceeds goals.

Incentives can make up for the limitations of fixed price and time and materials models, ensuring that your partner's motivations stay in line with your company's.

Shared Risk-Reward Pricing

Like the incentive-based pricing model, this pricing structure specifies a contracted rate and enables additional payments when specific objectives are achieved.

The key difference here is that the development of new products is funded jointly by the client and service provider, with the outsourcing partner sharing in the rewards for a defined period of time.

This innovative approach encourages your partners to develop ideas that add value to your business. However, be ready for rigorous oversight. The result of your partner's work may be difficult to measure, so you need to be prepared not only to enjoy the potential upsides (speed to market, increased revenue, customer satisfaction, etc.) but also to weather the downsides (delays and scope changes).

Finding the Sweet Spot between Quality and Cost

A focus on cost at the expense of quality comes with increased risks and the added stress of partnering with a less skilled, less stable, or less efficient outsourcing partner.

Software development that costs $100 per hour in the U.S. can be outsourced in most locations for just $55 per hour at an equivalent standard of quality. Less expensive options are available for companies on tighter budgets, but at that point you'll inevitably need to make some compromises.

As rates decline, quality can drop off exponentially. Unfortunately, we've seen this dynamic play out to a company's detriment too many times. Undercutting market rates by $10 an hour might win short-term kudos from your CFO, but it often results in sacrificing the level of skills and experience you need to ensure the quality and timeliness of your new product.

I always ask people who seek to cut rates what they're willing to give up in return. Less English competency? Less expertise? Less seniority? Less QA? No one ever gets something without giving in return. If the primary goal of your offshore strategy is cost savings, go for that model but pay the absolute most you can.

Through a proprietary analysis of cost vs. quality tradeoffs, Accelerance has identified a sweet spot—a range of rates from $40 to $90 per hour—that gives clients the confidence that their outsourcing partners will deliver cost-effective, high-performance solutions as promised. The chart below illustrates the differences between a partner in the "sweet spot" vs. a lower-cost partner.

Global Rates

$20 — $20-$40/hour — $40 — $40-$90/hour — $90

Offshore Body Shops	Enterprise-grade Offshore Partners
Low Cost Lowest-caliber talent Low maturity environment High outcome failure rate	Cost savings High quality talent comparable to domestic outsourced time Professional services level maturity Lower risk
Danger Zone	**The Sweet Spot**

Source: Accelerance Analysis 2022

For more context and detail, the table that follows lists the criteria we look for and rate against a spectrum of software engineering rates from $20 to $90 per hour. The descriptions highlight the differences between the "sweet spot" and "danger zone" rate ranges.

Hourly Rate of Software Engineers	
$20-$40/hour: "The Danger Zone"	**$40-$90/hour: "The Sweet Spot"**
Usually performs adequately in sales cycle: Project delivery team often does not speak or write fluent English with frequent communication issues.	Brings A+ English skills: Converses and communicates with confidence with all offshore team members; collaboration is much smoother.
Has minimal direct work experience with Western clients at the team level – may have exposure to smaller clients, often only one project.	Requires solid understanding of Western culture and practical work experience with teams – 95% of work is for Western clients.
Lacks track record and enterprise-grade attributes to gain certifications.	Possesses leading quality, industry and partner ecosystem certifications.
Follows instructions only as order takers with little collaboration or innovation; often unable to deliver to expected schedule, budget, and scope.	Engages resources who understand client needs and produce to their desired business outcomes, seeking to exceed expected performance.
Invests little to no effort for hiring more experienced resources and toward reducing turnover; employees are treated as commodities.	Recruits top-tier professionals with exceptional work experience and references, and invests in programs to attract and retain the best talent.

Detailed SLAs Lead to Greater Satisfaction

Service level agreements (SLAs) often don't get the attention they need in software development outsourcing contracts. This is a mistake because SLAs help you:

- Clarify performance expectations
- Ensure good customer service
- Establish measurable standards
- Outline remedies for non-performance

Some of the most common SLAs we see include:

System Availability
If your software runs in a cloud environment, or if you have a telco circuit or an internet circuit to your office, you probably have an SLA for uptime in your subscription agreement (e.g., 99.999% availability measured monthly). Similarly, if your outsourcing agreement includes infrastructure, platform, or software as a service components, take a page from the telco playbook and have an SLA that determines availability (e.g., percentage uptime, measured over a month).

> *Pro tip: You may care more about availability during your standard business hours. If end users don't require more, try to use an SLA metric focused on business-hour availability, not 24/7.*

System Responsiveness
Again, if you're using cloud infrastructure, platforms, or software your partner provides, an SLA should define how quickly the system responds. If your software development outsourcing partner is delivering a turn-key solution or major component, an SLA covering system response for the software they produce may be a good idea.

You can base this kind of SLA on one or more key user functions, or you can quantify the expected response time of a complex, predetermined SQL query as the "service" to be measured.

Partner Responsiveness
If you have a help desk service, your contract probably includes SLAs for response time (e.g., how long before a live agent responds to your ticket) and possibly mean time to resolution (e.g., typical time all tickets are resolved over a month).

Similarly, think about SLAs that create expectations of responsiveness from your partner. Examples might be:

- Time to respond to newly posted issues or bugs found during testing
- Time to estimate work-effort on proposed changes in scope
- Weekly deadline to post team progress, with an expectation of 100% compliance

Customer Satisfaction

Partners that provide some sort of support desk or help desk will often send users a "How did we do?" follow-up survey. You can require an SLA for scores that measure customer satisfaction (e.g., "95% positive feedback each month").

Agile Performance Metrics

In an Agile development project, you may want a commitment from your software outsourcing partner to periodically provide a report of software development metrics. The SLA could read something like: "Vendor will provide a monthly report on the following development metrics…"

Using an SLA in this way accomplishes two objectives:

- The partner is held accountable for continuous measurement and reporting; the reporting rhythm is your SLA
- The metrics the partner reports on, per the SLA, become baseline measurements for continuous improvement

Here are some of the metrics we recommend getting commitments for:

Lead Time

In software development, lead time is the length of time from concept to delivery. From project-to-project, or even epic-to-epic, you want to see an increase in the speed to deliver completed software.

Sprint Duration

Teams using Agile will have sprints measured in a few days, instead of months, for work timed in "phases" or "activities." Track the duration of your sprints and evaluate trends over time.

Sprint Volume
How many sprints are needed to complete a story? How many sprints are needed for a version? For each of these metrics, look for consistent volume (such as number of sprints produced) over time.

Variations in volume could mean you have a "lumpy" plan for a new feature rollout: too many sprints in one version, too few in another. A decline in the number of sprints produced might indicate that a recent developer change or reassignment caused a dip in team productivity.

Open/Close Rates
Measure how many production issues are reported and closed within a specific timeframe. Observe and act on trends, rather than establishing a hard-and-fast number, because there's really no right answer.

How to Structure Your SLAs

The commitments outlined in an SLA should cover all these essential elements in clear and specific detail:

- **Service**–The service or action the outsourcing partner will provide
- **Measurement**–The KPIs you'll use to quantify the service commitment
- **Interval**–How often each metric must be captured, such as every time the help desk is called, every month, etc.
- **Obligations**–Some SLAs have obligations that the client and the partner must fulfill to enforce the SLA, such as declaring an SLA violation to receive a penalty payment
- **Penalty**–This is the penalty for failure to comply with an SLA, otherwise known as an SLA violation. In software development outsourcing, an SLA penalty is often the loss of a "bonus payment" (or percentage) held in reserve by the client for a successfully completed project with all SLAs met

How Price and Performance Benchmarking Keeps You Right on the Money

To ensure that you don't end up paying too much for your software development, and that your outsourcing partners keep performing at high levels, it's important to include benchmarking provisions in your outsourcing contracts. Even if you have a good relationship with your development teams, benchmarking should be done by a professional consultant at least every two years to measure and compare the cost and performance of your partners against similar market suppliers.

I've seen too many companies miss out on savings and quality improvement opportunities by not initiating reviews as often as they should. Sometimes benchmarking shows that one or more of your processes needs to be re-engineered to improve performance, or that your service levels aren't as good as they could be.

Because benchmarking is a complex science, it's vital to choose a well-established, professional company that will make valid comparisons and conduct the process fairly and transparently. You and your outsourcing partner need to agree on data collection and sharing procedures, along with a comprehensive schedule that outlines any necessary remediation plans.

At a minimum, include the following benchmarking requirements in your outsourcing contracts right from the outset:

Periodic Benchmarking
As a general rule, you should be benchmarking every one to two years after your first year of working together. You should also specify the option to initiate additional benchmarking whenever a new service request is quoted. This allows you to test the market and ensure your provider isn't boosting rates to compensate for previously provided discounts.

Choice of Benchmarking Firms
Your contract should specify a shortlist of benchmarking firms that both parties are comfortable working with. It's also helpful to agree

on when to schedule the activity, ideally outside peak work volumes, taking into account the time needed for the service provider to make data available to resolve any issues.

Metric Clarity

Be very clear on what is fair to measure and compare. It's not reasonable (or useful) to compare the cost of an onshore software developer in the Bay Area to the cost of an offshore operation in Bangladesh, or set expectations that ignore the complexities of a challenging project.

For price benchmarking, baselines should include:

- Similar locations, as the cost of living has a big influence on market rate
- Similar-sized organizations, because global software houses have completely different cost structures than small, single-location, low-cost operators
- Similar industries, as applicable

For SLA benchmarking, the metrics should match the SLAs in your contract.

Remediation Plan

If a benchmarking report shows a discrepancy, both parties need to know how to proceed.

Breach of Contract Options

If rates and service levels are both unfavorable, you want to be able to do any of the following:

- Terminate the contract
- Request a service-level remediation plan with a timeframe for resolution
- Terminate the contract if the remediation plan doesn't work or isn't provided in a timely manner

Escape Clauses

Request provisions to protect the interests of both parties should a problem arise. These provisions often include:

- The ability to terminate the benchmarking process at any time (and start again with another company)
- A release, signed by the partner, for any losses suffered as a result of the benchmarking firm's findings
- A limit on how much current rates can be reduced
- An option that allows the client to replace the partner for underperforming services, if levels can't be brought up to an acceptable level

Evaluating Your Benchmarking Results

The benchmark report should be comprehensive and transparent, including details about the methodologies used, adjustments or normalizations made to data, and the attributes of organizations used for comparison. As soon as possible, the benchmarking report should be shared with your partner for consideration, feedback, and remediation (if necessary).

Typically, results in benchmarking reports are classified as favorable, competitive, and unfavorable:

- Favorable rates are less than 95% of the market rate, and favorable SLAs are within the top 5% of results being achieved by similar organizations
- Competitive rates are between 95% and 105% of the market rate, and competitive SLAs are within the top 5%–10% of results being achieved by similar organizations
- Unfavorable rates are more than 105% of the market rate, and unfavorable SLAs are below the top 10% of results achieved by similar organizations

If your outsourcing partner is hitting the sweet spot with competitive or favorable rates, and providing a high level of service, you can file away your outsourcing contract for another couple of years, or until it comes up for renewal.

But what if the benchmarking report shows that performance has slipped, or that you've been paying above the market rate?

First, hear your partner out. There may be structural inefficiencies that can be remedied, or a problematic sub-contracting arrangement that will take a little time to resolve. No one wins if you get into a heated dispute, especially if you want to move forward and maintain a positive working relationship. Most partners will act in good faith, and should have a remediation plan in place within a few weeks.

The table on the next page shows you what to do in different situations, based on your benchmarking results.

New Ways to Look at Benchmarking

While the ubiquity of the cloud has loosened the need to enter multi-year contracts, good relationships can still last for years, or even decades. And clients still need a mechanism to prove that prices are within market rates and that value is increasing as the relationship evolves.

One of the things that benchmarking professionals should look at is the level of innovation that an outsourcing partner provides to its client. If an outsourcing partner isn't taking advantage of the latest technological developments, the newest ways of working, and other efficiencies that others are using for competitive advantage, then the client is, on some level, paying too much for services rendered and should have some recourse.

The overhead of running an engineering operation has improved dramatically with the concepts of DevOps and automated testing, for example, which have enabled a greater degree of certainty around test results and their impact on the production system. It's only fair to make sure your outsourcing partner is using those kinds of innovations to provide better value to you, so you really should include a provision in your benchmarking agreement that allows your partner to demonstrate how it's using innovation on your behalf.

In my view, even cultural and relationship aspects should be measured through benchmarking. Are your outsourced team members just telling you yes, or are they really challenging you? Are they asking clarifying questions, probing more, and deepening their understanding of your business model? Do they make recommendations that improve your results? Do they appreciate and accommodate your ways of working?

Actions to Take Based on Benchmarking Results

	Service Levels		
Rates	**Favorable**	**Competitive**	**Unfavorable**
Favorable	**Recommendation:** No change anticipated	**Recommendation:** No change anticipated	**Recommendation:** Client should request a service-level remediation plan, typically with a timeframe for resoltuion
Competitive	**Recommendation:** No change anticipated	**Recommendation:** No change anticipated	**Recommendation:** Client should request a service-level remediation plan, typically with a timeframe for resoltuion
Unfavorable	**Recommendation:** Client will seek a variation to the contract to maintain performance and reduce cost, or reduce service levels to enable costs	**Recommendation:** Rates must be reduced to benchmark level, usually with immediate effect	**Recommendation:** Urgent action is required

The kind of harmony that comes from conscientious and engaged team members, along with an agreed-upon way of working, can create a powerful efficiency dividend that should be encouraged and rewarded. This area of benchmarking is very underexplored and underutilized today, but I think we'll be seeing more metrics around relationship maintenance and relationship improvement in the near future.

In an ideal situation, benchmarking should be a reason to celebrate the success of how far you've come with your outsourcing partner, and what you've achieved in terms of working together and staying in sync.

*****

Now that you know everything your business needs to get ready for outsourcing, it's time to make multinational management a reality at your organization. In the next chapter, we'll discuss what it takes to find a perfect-fit partner for your projects.

GUEST EXPERT SPOTLIGHT

RICH WANDEN

From management consulting to sales, Rich Wanden has worked with companies—including EY, Deloitte, CSC, LogicaCMG, and Tech Mahindra—that make training and investing in their people a top priority. He brings his passion for helping teams do what's right for customers in his role as Chief Customer Success Officer at Accelerance.

No One Enters a Bad Deal on Purpose

Decent firms will accommodate your culture and work the way you need them to.

When structuring outsourcing deals, business leaders often fail to understand the consequences of what they're choosing. Each different deal structure requires certain prerequisites to ensure that work gets done the way you need it to.

For example, setting up a captive entity requires a lot of overhead and management, and you may need to fly several people over to make sure things are running smoothly. Staff augmentation is much simpler on the face of it, but that too comes with its own set of challenges. Your hiring managers, for example, must be adept at picking the right people—especially if all they get from a so-called "partner" are a bunch of resumes and Zoom appointments.

Before entering any agreement, it's important to gain clarity over what you're getting and what you need to give. If you need to give more than you're able to, it's time to find another partner. On the other hand, if you understand your roles and responsibilities and are willing to take them on, then you shouldn't have too many surprises down the road. It's far better to understand all the nuances of an agreement upfront, instead of trying to make a bad situation better later.

Evaluating different outsourcing models and partners really depends on what you've prepared for, how much money and other resources you can or need to invest, and your level of outsourcing maturity. To gain experience, critical learning, and some quick victories, it may be wise to start with a simple arrangement and work up to one that gives you more control.

Because certain things will make any outsourcing arrangement successful outside of the specific legal parameters, make sure you're working with enterprise-grade outsourcing partners. These firms are highly sophisticated when it comes to information security, employee confidentiality, and Western ways of working. Creating great software is in their DNA, and because they're technologists first they'll likely become major contributors to the quality of your products.

These types of decent firms don't walk into arrangements with new customers hoping that they'll work. They know they can work because they've done it for others and they're willing to outline how it's going to work for you.

Don't be shy about telling a prospective partner how you work and how you need them to accommodate you. It's important to outline the day-to-day processes that will underpin your relationship, and to feel confident that you're getting the service leadership you need to evolve your partnership.

Hoping that everything's going to go perfectly well is not a strategy, so take some extra time to spell things out in advance. I don't think anybody ever intends to enter a bad arrangement that's going to fail, but sometimes misunderstandings arise due to a lack of inquiry upfront. Surfacing potential issues—as part of figuring out who you could be working with and how that would work for you—is vital to getting a successful deal.

Most contracts I've seen in the U.S. lean very heavily toward definitions and punitive damages. Unlike contracts in other parts of the world, they tend not to talk much about facilitation, remediation, ways of working together, and other governance issues. In other words, they're very short on what happens when something happens.

If possible, try to document the structures and processes that will support the team so it can achieve the desired outcome. It's worth the effort, especially if you're trying to mobilize dozens of developers and engineers to build the next generation of your product.

I'll close this section with some advice on price. English philosopher John Ruskin famously said:

> *"It's unwise to pay too much, but it's worse to pay too little. When you pay too much, you lose a little money—that's all. When you pay too little, you sometimes lose everything, because the thing you bought was incapable of doing the thing it was bought to do. The common law of business balance prohibits paying a little and getting a lot—it can't be done. If you deal with the lowest bidder, it is well to add something for the risk you run, and if you do that you will have enough to pay for something better."*

When you enter any outsourcing agreement, you want the best and brightest people you can afford. So make sure you choose a partner that values its employees, pays them well, and gives them exciting work. This generally leads to low attrition rates and a higher caliber of developer—two things that will benefit your projects. If your prospective partners aren't willing to verify their attrition rates or let you talk with their employees, don't sign anything that you can't get out of quickly.

You may love the salesperson or the CEO at the company you want to partner with, but the people you do the deal with aren't the ones who'll be developing your software. If you dig deep into the day-to-day processes that will manifest successful outcomes you'll have a more successful outsourcing experience, however you choose to structure it.

"If you want to go fast, go alone. If you want to go far, go together."
—*African Proverb*

CHAPTER 6

REALIZING YOUR OWN GLOBALLY DISTRIBUTED REALITY

Once you've established your readiness for multinational management via outsourcing, it's time to make it actually happen. The goal, as you'll see in a later chapter, is to build a worldwide tech value network that can give you the resilience you need to get through any business crisis, rapidly bring your next big ideas to life, and keep improving your software offerings to the delight of your customers and the chagrin of your competitors.

Just as thoroughly as you assessed your own business, you'll want to do a similar exercise with potential outsourcing partners. Knowing how to identify and evaluate what we call "right-fit" partners is critical to the success of any outsourcing project.

In this chapter, I'll share our proven due diligence process that draws on decades of experience vetting the world's most qualified software development firms. We've used it to research more than 8,000 companies in more than 40 countries, and when you understand the criteria we use to pick the best of the best you'll be able to tap into quality skills and expertise from around the world.

In a global market awash with software development firms of varying quality and reputation, it's never been more important to have an objective process for finding the firms and people who can see your projects through to successful completion. Thousands of potential partners may look good on paper or on a website, but when you dig a little deeper you'll realize that many of those would be far too risky to work with.

Lots of software development organizations have been set up to capitalize on the outsourcing trend, just to make a quick buck. Many of these operate with no hiring or training standards, no oversight or support, no guaranteed employee retention or continuity, and no insurance. These types of companies are notorious for being more concerned about putting butts in seats than building a culture of excellence and innovation. The best talent is more likely to walk out of these organizations, and if you get tricked into hiring a shop like this you're likely to be stuck with second-rate developers. As the saying goes, may the buyer beware.

All too often, we've acquired clients after breakdowns in their outsourcing partner relationships led to costly delays and products delivered without critical features. In one instance, the wasted time and effort cost one of our clients more than $1 million by the time they came to us. The software development company held the client's code hostage until the contract was paid in full, and the software that was finally delivered didn't even meet specifications. It was an ugly mess that could have been avoided with a little prep work and an understanding of what makes one firm a partner and another firm a disaster waiting to happen. I encourage you to study this chapter so you know what to look for.

Finding Your Right-Fit Partners

Cultural and language barriers, a lack of accountability, mismatched capabilities, and a lack of size alignment between clients and outsourcing partners are issues that can derail an outsourcing engagement early on.

According to one study of companies that had engaged outsourcing partners, a lack of shared intellectual capital was the main culprit in outsourcing relationships gone bad. Intellectual capital is the domain and technical knowledge of a team, as well as its social skills. In other words, it's the sum of an organization's capability and experience. The lesson to be learned is that if you're unclear about exactly what an outsourcing partner can bring to your project, avoid the relationship at all costs.

Through the past decades, we've found that the best software development partners are first and foremost business leaders and thought leaders, not simply order takers who deliver code. You might end up paying a little more for smarter, more professional talent—and you may have to adapt to a more lateral management style (more about that in the next chapter)—but it'll still be a lot less expensive than hiring locally and you'll gain added value from fast, efficient workflows, team stability, and the potential for product improvements you might never have thought of on your own.

Multinational management, done right, requires hiring highly professional, enterprise-grade partners. Because certified global software development firms can easily integrate talent into an existing team with minimum disruption, these partners command a slight premium.

Instead of settling for a group of low-performing, order-taking developers, do the due diligence required to find proactive problem solvers who'll deliver results beyond your expectations. It'll make your job as a multinational manager a lot easier, giving you more time to focus on higher-level issues instead of wasting time on day-to-day irritations.

At Accelerance, our partner vetting methodology considers criteria across many different areas, including team size, cultural fit, company track record, and relevant industry experience. Each certified development firm in our global network must pass a stringent, 500-point checklist. Once they pass that hurdle, we go the extra mile and conduct on-site assessments to bring our clients the world's largest, most thoroughly vetted software outsourcing network.

While we take pride in the level of sophistication we bring to the partner evaluation process, I'll let you in on a little secret. Choosing the right outsourcing partner really boils down to three essential issues:

- How well they communicate
- How well they collaborate
- How well they complete projects on time

If you focus your due diligence efforts in the partner selection process on these areas, I can virtually guarantee that it'll make all the difference in the success of your engagement.

Size Matters

This single tip will save you a lot of time and effort right from the start in your search for a right-fit outsourcing partner: Only work with partners that are large enough to scale and small enough to care.

A partner that's too small may not have sufficient resources to complete your project on time or may lack the bench strength to cover your needs.

Partners that are too large can also be a mismatch if your project isn't "big enough to matter." You could easily get ignored in this situation, or you could end up not being able to establish ongoing relationships with the same people.

A good rule of thumb is to make sure your engagement represents no less than 5% and no more than 20% of your partner's revenue base.

That being said, I'm going to cover seven partnership success factors you should assess before signing any contracts. Most of these success factors relate to the three bullet points above, but it's also important to consider rates, expenses, and geopolitical issues before stepping into a high-stakes relationship.

After a short description of each success factor, I'll share a list of questions to ask so you can do your own partner vetting at a high confidence level. I recommend asking the questions over a Zoom call that you can record and look back on, but you can also package up your questions in an email and review written responses. Either way, the answers you'll get will provide useful insights into the candidates you're considering.

Seven Partnership Success Factors

The success of our due diligence process lies in taking a carefully planned, step-by-step approach to vetting potential partners that covers their experience and qualifications, technical expertise, rates, culture, communication skills, and commitment to intellectual property protection, as well as an analysis of geopolitical factors that may interfere with your relationship in the future.

Success Factor #1: Experience and Qualifications

There's nothing more important than knowing that the outsourcing partner you engage is highly accomplished and can take on every aspect of your project, from requirement identification and planning to development and testing.

Against these criteria, you'll want to carefully investigate each potential candidate's depth of experience, ability to ramp up quickly, ratio of junior to senior team members they recommend for your project (more senior people is usually better), and stability as a business.

Be sure to check at least three references that show positive experiences with projects as close to yours as possible. Ideal references are from people in your own country, who you can have a detailed, nuanced conversation with. Case studies and customer testimonials on a website are great, but you should never take them at face value.

It can be a plus if a potential partner has experience in the industry you work in, but don't get too fixated on that. It's much more important that your partner demonstrate an ability to complete similarly scoped projects on time and according to the highest quality standards.

Recruiting Strategies and Human Capital Investment

Excellent recruiting is part of the service a world-class software outsourcing partner provides. Your partner should be able to bring you qualified candidates, so you can quickly review their resumes to confirm that they'll be valuable contributors to your project.

The best partners have a deep pipeline of highly qualified candidates, with a clear process for interviewing, hiring, and retention. Be sure to ask questions about the talent pool they'll be drawing from to put together your remote team and confirm that they maintain a bench of developers ready to jump in if someone leaves.

Some of the partners we work with provide their talent pool with English language training and certification in technologies like Oracle,

Salesforce, Amazon Web Services, SAP, and Microsoft. Others pay for scrum teams to visit each other from time to time, especially during ramp up or if they need training around regulatory requirements. In your vetting process, look for cues that tell you which potential partners are ready, willing, and eager to invest in a long-term relationship.

Due Diligence Questions

1. Can you describe your company history?
2. How long have you been in business? *(well-established companies have been operating for 5+ years)*
3. How is your company organized?
4. How many clients do you currently have?
5. Can you describe the size and scope of your client projects?
6. Which of your current or past clients are most like us?
7. How do you measure and manage customer satisfaction?
8. Can you provide three or more client references?
9. How many locations do you have? Where are they?
10. How many full-time employees do you have?
11. How do you recruit, qualify, and onboard new developers?
12. Do you do background checks when hiring new employees?
13. What kind of NDAs do your employees sign?
14. What was your attrition rate for the past year?
15. How does your attrition rate compare to similar companies?
16. What are your employee retention strategies?
17. How will you handle and minimize attrition on my team?
18. How developed is your country as an outsourcing destination?
19. What are the current trends and outlook?

Success Factor #2: Technical Expertise

Specific technical competence is just as important as a potential partner's overall professionalism and track record, so it's important to verify skill levels and capabilities beyond verbal assurances. Push to see certifications and examples of projects like yours that have been completed for other clients.

Access to technical skills is often cited by IT executives as the greatest barrier to their department's success. One of the key benefits of managing outsourced talent is that they can bring you immediate access to experience with leading and emerging technologies that could take your company years to develop or duplicate in-house, so you want to make sure your partner can rise to the occasion.

Begin by identifying the top three technical skills your project requires to make the greatest impact. Before you can determine what your partner can deliver, you have to understand what you need. Sometimes this can be a chicken-or-egg kind of scenario if you're new to software development or aren't up to speed on the latest technologies, but if you can do your homework and create a list of required engineering or development skills, it'll be a lot easier to eliminate companies that aren't worth talking to and create a shortlist of potential partners that meet your criteria.

In addition to sharing your list of technical requirements when you reach out to prospective firms, give them an overview of the software you want to create, tell them how many developers you think you need on your team, and outline your long-term vision and goals.

Insist on Specialists

While generalists are valuable for their broad knowledge, specialists increase the value of your software and your outsourcing investment. Outsourcing providers that specialize in your technical requirements should be at the top of your shortlist for consideration.

Ask potential partners for proof of current certifications in both established and emerging technologies, and keep in mind that teams with a mix of junior, mid-level, and senior developers usually perform best. A lower-cost team of all junior developers will lack the experience you need to be productive, while hiring only experienced senior developers will cost you more and may cause teamwork issues.

Due Diligence Questions

1. Why do you consider yourself to be an expert in the software technologies we require?
2. How many of your internal resources and clients are currently using the same technology stack?
3. What current technical certifications do your developers hold?
4. What is your QA approach?
5. Can you describe your approach to Agile development?

Success Factor #3: Rates and Expenses

Outsourcing has a well-deserved reputation for being highly cost-effective. In most cases, you get more value for your dollar by managing people offshore or nearshore than you can from managing people in-house or through local consultants.

In the last chapter we talked about the “sweet spot” rate range of between $40 and $90 per hour, so it’s good to have that in mind when you’re vetting potential partners. Remember that it’s always important to look beyond the rates you’re quoted and carefully consider the actual value you’re getting for your money.

For example, you’ll want to get a sense of whether your potential partners are aligned on how many people are needed to complete your project. Does one suggest a five-member team while another recommends 30 developers? You might think that the higher number is an attempt to rip you off, but sometimes it's a mistake to limit headcount if it puts your deadline at risk or results in low quality work.

You'll also want to compare your quoted rates to the average range for the geographical region you're looking at, based on like-for-like software engagements. Be ready to recognize when costs are abnormally above or below normal, or when something just doesn't feel right.

Rates can vary considerably, not only by region but also by skill level, experience, the specific technology stack involved, and the length of commitment required. Pay close attention to everything your quotes include and don't include.

Total Cost of Engagement

Rates are important, but the total cost of engagement (TCE) is a better measure of the value you're getting for your money.

When hiring your own developers in-house, for example, your costs include a base rate plus taxes, health benefits, retirement plans, bonuses, vacation time, overhead, etc. When you outsource, many of those costs are significantly reduced or disappear entirely and the savings can really add up.

On the other hand, travel and other expenses might eat up some of these savings. In addition, some outsourcing partners may include a "risk factor charge" for deals that aren't brokered through a trusted advisor like Accelerance. This may increase your quote by up to 50%, so be sure to ask about it and try to negotiate it down.

Most outsourcing experts suggest adding about 20% on top of the price you're quoted to determine the total cost of a partner engagement.

It's a good rule of thumb, but don't forget to factor in what the more intangible benefits of your outsourcing relationship—such as onboarding and offboarding flexibility, rapid access to specific skill sets, and vertical experience—might be worth to you. You may find that the peace of mind you get from working with a company that's more expensive is more valuable than saving a few pennies.

Due Diligence Questions

1. What other expenses do clients like us typically incur when they work with you?
2. How often should we meet in person and what should we budget for travel?
3. What intangible benefits of working with you should we include in our cost/value equation?
4. Are you including a "risk factor charge" in your quote? How is that determined and is there any flexibility there?

Success Factor #4: Cultural Nuances

The national culture of an outsourcing partner can have a big impact on the success of your project, but their business culture and software development culture should also be considered as part of your vetting process. A good cultural fit—on all levels—can make or break your relationship.

Fear of differences can be a hindrance, so it's important to go into any outsourcing relationship with curiosity, appreciation, and an open mind. Different cultures bring in new and fresh ways of thinking, and if you embrace the differences you might be surprised by the opportunities that come your way. As I mentioned in the Introduction about my Peace Corps experience in Costa Rica, interacting with people from different countries and backgrounds can be one of the most rewarding aspects of your multinational management engagements.

For these interactions to go as smoothly as possible, however, both parties must have some understanding of how the other party thinks and behaves. It's not necessary for one side to completely adapt to the other, but it is necessary for both sides to recognize and embrace the other's cultural customs.

On your side, it's important to learn as much as you can about your outsourcing provider's country, region, way of life, manners and behaviors, and even some of their language if you can. You certainly need to know enough to avoid inadvertently offending people you want to work with.

Being courteous and respectful goes a long way toward building trust. All people mess up from time to time, and if you do end up making a faux pas you'll want to apologize as soon as possible. Some people are lighthearted about things like this, but others can take them very seriously so you must be sincere about it. Your investment in understanding your partners will be critical to the success of your project and will pay huge dividends.

At the same time, it's important to choose partners with a proven track record of working with Western companies. Even if a partner's national culture is vastly different from your own, are there people on the team who understand the needs and wants of Western companies and their customers? Have senior employees studied or worked in the U.S., Canada, Western Europe, or Australia?

Assess the Business Culture

Beyond a prospective partner's national culture, be sure to look at the cultural aspects of how they run their business on a day-to-day basis. Even little details can indicate how well an outsourced software development firm will work with you and your organization:

- Are their facilities attractive and well kept?
- Are meetings with you collaborative, creative, and positive?
- Are your contacts engaged with you and committed to your success?

It's important to ask these questions of your own business, too: If you hold a third party to a higher standard than you hold yourself, you'll likely be the reason a project goes south.

In the discovery phase of your outsourcing journey, be sure to define parameters for how you expect work to get done. If you expect your partners to follow the Agile methodology, for example, you'll want to communicate that upfront and know that they're comfortable working that way.

You'll also want to seek out partners that put their strategic focus on innovation and establish incentives and rewards for their most creative employees. The best engineers and developers want to be a part of a company that allows them to think and grow, and companies that encourage this grow, too.

Due Diligence Questions

1. What experience do you have working with Western clients?
2. Have any of your business leaders and employees studied in the U.S. or other Western countries?
3. Do any of your business leaders and employees have work experience in the U.S. or other Western countries?
4. How would you describe your company culture?
5. What are your company's core values?
6. What values do you look for in your employees?
7. Describe your client ramp-up process, including staffing, knowledge transfer, and project metrics.
8. Can you describe a client project that went wrong and what you did to fix it?

Success Factor #5: Communication Skills

Communication is another important contributor to the success or failure of multinational management engagements. If you can't communicate instructions, or if your prospective partner can't understand them, it's not worth forming a partnership. For a relationship to grow and a project to stay on track, both parties must set clear expectations, overcome language barriers, and communicate clearly and consistently.

Unless you're proficient in the language of your outsourced team members, it's important to find partners who have at least a conversational level of English proficiency. Senior members need to clearly understand the requirements of your engagement before they're able to build your product. You don't have to demand English language skills that are equivalent to a native speaker's, but you should feel comfortable that language-driven misunderstandings will be kept to a minimum.

In addition to overcoming language barriers, make sure you understand the norms for communication in your outsourcing partner's country. Even English-speaking nations such as the U.S., the UK, and Australia all have different communication styles and idiosyncrasies. What you might consider rude, odd, or confusing may be perfectly normal in another culture. The key to bridging these gaps is mutual respect and a genuine appreciation of your differences.

Communicate Early, Often, and Face to Face

Open communication is extremely important in any language because it keeps everyone aligned on important details and ensures that everyone's needs and expectations are met from start to finish. Make sure your potential partner is open to a formal cadence of touch-base meetings and the use of task-oriented collaboration tools, such as Asana, Wrike, and Basecamp.

Frequent status reports are a great way to update business leaders on the progress of your project, so make sure your potential partners will provide professional reporting on a consistent basis. Also make sure that you establish a mechanism for identifying issues as soon as they arise, with a clear process for assigning responsibility and tracking progress through resolution.

Using video calls, especially when you're vetting potential partners and in the beginning of your outsourcing relationships, can help you read body language and interpret levels of understanding. If the visual cues you're getting don't align with what's being said, you can try to rephrase things or ask questions that help clarify your conversations.

While in-person visits aren't practical for everyone, they can be incredibly important if you're hoping to develop a long-term relationship with a partner. Traveling to a different country can also be an incentive for people on your team. If you can make it happen and want travel to be part of the engagement, be sure to pick a partner that's open to having you visit and that's located in an area with the infrastructure to accommodate your visiting team members.

Due Diligence Questions

1. How do you measure the level of your employees' English ability?
2. What collaboration processes and tools do you typically use?
3. How do you help keep everyone aligned on shared goals?
4. How do you accommodate time zone differences?
5. Can team members travel to visit us? Can we visit you?
6. When are the best times of year to visit?

Success Factor #6: Intellectual Property Protection

Within the U.S., it's customary to ask employees and contractors to sign non-disclosure agreements (NDAs) that prevent them from sharing confidential information or intellectual property (IP). Offshore, however, different countries have different laws that could put your IP at risk.

If IP is something you need to protect, you'll want to eliminate—or at least mitigate—your risk by only working with partners who understand the importance of confidentiality. Building software that requires unique algorithms or proprietary coding research can put your IP at greater risk, so make sure that your potential partners can offer adequate levels of protection:

- Technical protection–firewalls, virtual desktops, VPNs, encryption
- Legal protection–copyrights assigned properly, NDAs, patent protection
- Physical protection–locked rooms, key card access, security guards, partitioned teams

Be sure to discuss these issues before entering into any agreement, and make sure you're comfortable with the level of protection being offered. Specific IP protocols should be clearly outlined in any contracts with outsourcing partners.

In your early discussions, be explicit about copyright ownership and any other rights you have and how they'll be protected. Find out, for example, if you can limit the information you share so work can get done without having to divulge valuable trade secrets. Try to either prohibit the use of subcontractors or ensure that any subcontractors hired will be governed by the same rules as your direct partner.

You may have to get creative, but an above-board partner will respect your rights and work with you to find a solution. The best software development companies will fiercely protect your intellectual property, not as a favor to you but as a professional commitment to world-class service.

Due Diligence Questions

1. How will you protect my source code and other intellectual property?
2. Where will my data be stored during development?

3. What business continuity and resilience protocols have you put in place?
4. Do you carry professional indemnity and public liability insurance?
5. How do you comply with legislation related to the Office of Foreign Assets Control (OFAC), anti-corruption and money laundering, and human trafficking?

Success Factor #7: Geopolitical Events

As we discussed in the first chapter about disruption, no one really knows what's going to happen next in a volatile world. Several elements of this particular success factor are largely out of anyone's control, but a little research on current events could save you from making a big mistake.

Current geopolitical realities can help you decide whether or not to do business in a certain part of the world, especially if you and your team members are planning to visit your partner on occasion. Some countries require visas that aren't always easy to get, for example, so be sure to understand the process. You'll also want to do some research about how safe it is to travel in and out of a particular country.

Another thing to keep in mind is that not all countries have the same views regarding criminal behavior. I remember one famous case back in the 1990s, in which a student from the U.S. was sentenced to caning in Singapore for stealing a road sign. Be sure you understand how civil law is handled in countries where you and other people from your in-house team may be visiting for business.

Knowledge of the local legal system will also help you draw up contracts that are legally valid and protect your intellectual property, as we discussed above. A good safeguard is to work with partners that have a subsidiary in your home country. That way, your contract could be under U.S., UK, or Australian jurisdiction and you can make payments to your offshore partners in your own country.

One of the big buzzwords in outsourcing today is friendshoring, or allyshoring. The idea here is that it's much better to outsource work to people in countries that are political and economic allies over countries that are enemies or potential enemies. Many businesspeople want to stay out of politics, but sometimes it's wise to consider whether or not the money you're paying your outsourcing partner, or the IP you're sharing with them, could be used against your home country one day.

Political Stability and Natural Disasters

While these components are largely unpredictable, companies with relatively low risk tolerance should factor them into any outsourcing partnership decision. Check for signs that the current government structure will remain stable, or that the nearby volcano isn't going to start erupting when your project begins

Due Diligence Questions

1. How stable is your country's economy?
2. Does your country have good relations with Western governments?
3. What geopolitical factors are likely to affect the stability of your country over the next few years?

Time Zone Considerations

While the geographical distance between you and your outsourcing partners is less of an issue now that video conferencing, document sharing, and online collaboration tools are readily available, time zone differences can influence which partners you decide to work with.

Some U.S. companies prefer to work with partners in Latin America because of the amount of overlap in each other's workday. Costa Rica, for example, is only two hours behind New York, and Argentina is only one hour ahead.

Outsourcing Failure Story: How Wrong Can It Go?

I know of an engineering Vice President who spent five painstaking months (at about $15K per month) traveling the world in search of a partner. He investigated companies in India, China, and South America, and ended up selecting a U.S.-owned vendor with operations in China. The vendor was in the process of acquiring a second team of programmers who were perfect for this VP's needs.

When the team acquisition fell through at the last minute, the partner assigned a junior team to the VP's project. The programmers' English skills were limited, which made communication both difficult and inefficient, but their programming skills were even worse.

Because of the 16-hour time difference with China, managers in the U.S. spent many late nights emailing detailed instructions (and even pseudo code) and answering questions by phone.

Severe morale problems emerged among the U.S. staff, along with missed deadlines and extreme employee frustration that eventually elevated the issue to the board level.

Finally, after a long six-month learning curve the Chinese team became more efficient, but the damage was done. Despite all the travel and research, the VP had made a big mistake and was forced to resign.

Other U.S. companies like the idea of partnering with teams farther offshore, because while one part of the team is sleeping the other part of the team can be getting things done.

In either case, working with people in different time zones requires a fair amount of schedule coordination and sometimes a little personal sacrifice to keep projects moving. This is something you should discuss with your in-house team, because the last thing you want to do is upset good employees by asking them to spend late nights or Sunday mornings working with your outsourcing partners.

Decisions about how teams fit together across time zones can be extremely disrupting or extremely empowering, so make sure to consider the consequences of all your options.

One More Note about Travel

We'll talk more about the benefits of travel when it comes to outsourcing engagements in the next chapter, but if you can visit your top outsourcing partner candidates before you sign a contract, I highly recommend it. Nothing beats meeting in person to confirm and celebrate your choice—or to realize that you and a potential partner just aren't a good fit.

Outsourcing Success Story: Getting Over a Fear of Outsourcing

Using our due diligence process, CSG International found a perfect-fit partner in Mexico. The Colorado-based provider of business support systems to the telecommunications industry was impacted by the tech skills shortage, but IT leaders at the company had a poor experience with outsourcing in the past and were hesitant to try it again.

An urgent need for leading e-commerce applications that could optimize customer engagement led a nervous team of executives to us. After assessing their specific needs, we matched CSG with a certified partner that provided several teams of 10 developers each, all of whom had deep expertise in Scaled Agile Framework (SAFe).

The partner was able to meet fluctuating capacity needs and brought solid industry experience with communications and entertainment service providers to the table.

Spending time at a potential partner's location will give you a chance to fall in love with the national culture and provide valuable insights into how the partner's company operates, from their business culture and infrastructure to team morale and English language skills. What's more, getting there once from wherever you're based will give you a good idea how easy or difficult it will be to travel there every few months in the future.

Accelerating the Due Diligence Process

While our due diligence process is extremely thorough and can look rather daunting, it doesn't have to take long to vet a substantial number of potential partners. For one thing, many will not respond and others will stop talking to you when you start asking questions that could reveal that they don't take their business as seriously as they should.

You don't want to work with those companies anyway, so when they bow out of the process it's a blessing. On the other hand, since competition for software engineers and other technology talent is at a fever pitch these days, you don't want to create a protracted interview process that will turn potential partners away from your project. Development companies weighing multiple offers aren't interested in wasting their time with a potential client who can't make a quick decision.

The vetting process works both ways, so if you like the look of a potential partner after the first interview and their references check out, clearly signal your interest and make an offer as soon as you can. Obviously, partners will give you more leeway if you're planning to meet them in person, but in general it's a good idea to strike while the iron is hot in a seller's market.

Competition is fierce, especially for the best outsourcing partner organizations, and you don't want to miss out on a great relationship by hemming and hawing too much. Do your best to secure your preferred candidate swiftly and think of it as a working interview.

In return for a fast-tracked engagement, partners that are above board should be willing to negotiate a trial period of two to four weeks, so you can assess the quality of their work and see if they fit in with your internal team members before making a long-term commitment. Most of these agreements include a clause specifying that no payment will be made for substandard work done during the trial.

Going through the due diligence process may give you one clear winner from the potential partners that responded to your initial inquiry, answered your questions, and provided references. More likely than not, however, you'll have three or four potential partners that seem promising. At this point, you'll have to trust your gut and strike a deal as quickly as possible.

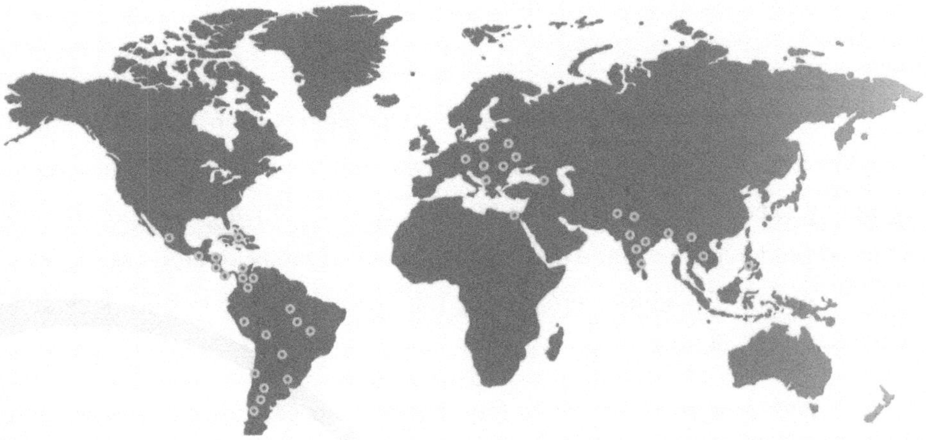

Great Developers Are Everywhere

Look beyond the limitations of borders to find a high level of technology skills and expertise around the globe. Outsourcing is possible anywhere there are smart people—which is pretty much everywhere. My team at Accelerance has identified quality talent across Latin America, Central and Eastern Europe, Africa, and Asia.

Latin America	Argentina, Bolivia, Brazil, Chile, Colombia, Costa Rica, El Salvador, Honduras, Mexico, Panama, Peru, Puerto Rico, Uruguay
Europe	Armenia, Bosnia, Bulgaria, Croatia, Hungary, Montenegro, Poland, Portugal, Romania, Serbia, Slovenia, Ukraine
South Asia	Bangladesh, India, Pakistan, Sri Lanka
Asia	China, Philippines, Vietnam
Africa	Egypt

Outsourcing Success Story: Seamless Integration with a Nearshore Partner

AdRoll is a leading performance advertising platform with more than 500,000 active advertisers worldwide. With rapidly growing digital needs, company executives wanted to implement a new software sourcing model so they could quickly expand their development capacity and tech skills. Specifically, AdRoll IT leaders were looking for a nearshore team to work closely with their internal team.

With an eye toward a long-term partnership, Executive Vice President of Engineering Patrick Mee (Guest Expert Spotlight Chapter 2) sought a Latin American partner that would fit well with their culture and workday timing. Lacking prior outsourcing experience, Mee also wanted an advisor to help coach, launch, and manage the team as it ramped up to meet development goals.

We matched AdRoll with a partner in Argentina that had a deep talent pool. The firm could provide qualified team members with certified skillsets right away and add new people as needed. What's more, the partner's Agile development approach allowed for a full cycle of software development in a timesaving, collaborative, and effective way.

This flexible outsourcing capability completely transformed AdRoll's development function, allowing the IT department to expand and optimize quality development resources significantly faster than most organizations.

The outsourced team became a seamless extension of AdRoll's internal team. Thanks to the collaborative nature of the partner's business culture, the perfect-fit team grew from five developers to more than 40 in the first year, giving AdRoll executives the resources they needed to completely elevate their product experience.

GUEST EXPERT SPOTLIGHT

TROY HILTBRAND

Troy Hiltbrand is currently Vice President of IT and Compensation Strategy at Amare Global, The Mental Wellness Company. A strategic IT executive, his core strengths lie in assembling and leading diverse global, Agile teams from Colombia, Brazil, Uruguay, Argentina, Mexico, the Philippines, Canada, and China, utilizing data, technology, and business process optimization to boost revenue and streamline costs.

Smart People Don't Make a Team—Heart Does

It's amazing how much more dedicated people can be to a project when team members have bonded on a personal basis.

When I was brought in as Chief Digital Officer at Kyani (now part of Amare Global) in 2015, my mandate was to digitally transform the organization but I had no staff. My counterpart in IT, the CIO, had his hands full with our e-commerce platform, cybersecurity concerns, help desk operations, and other day-to-day issues, and didn't have the capacity to execute on the vision I had for our worldwide network of commission-based distributors.

Utilizing international resources was something I had long been interested in, so I started to investigate nearshoring options. That's when I met Andy Hilliard and his team at Accelerance. They proposed three partners, and I talked with all of them about the technology they offered, the way they worked, and their cultures.

I decided to go with a company in Colombia because they really seemed to understand how to make a nearshoring relationship work from a cultural standpoint. It didn't hurt that they also understood Agile development very well and knew how to do it as a repeatable, scalable process.

Choosing that partner was the best decision I ever made. I've learned so many things from them, including how integrity and trust make a relationship flourish and how to create a bridge between cultures.

One example of this came when we decided to do some retrospectives and daily meetings completely in Spanish. My Spanish is pretty basic, but when it was my turn to share my progress I did it in Spanish and showed them that I'm as fallible as anyone else. When the team saw that I was willing to be open and vulnerable, they knew they could be vulnerable as well, especially if they were nervous about their English. I can't tell you how much it deepens a relationship when both sides open themselves up to say, "Hey, I don't know everything about you but I'm willing to learn."

One of the most important things I recommend to people considering an international, blended team relationship is to start it off in person. We spent a week with our new partner in Colombia, and it really did make a difference. While I think you can do your selection process without visiting, once you have a team that's yours you really need to be there with them.

During COVID I kicked off another partnership in Brazil over Zoom. It was okay, and we got creative about using Zoom in an interactive way, but the relationship improved significantly when I finally got to see the team in person.

To be honest, face to face is where the magic happens. I happened to be traveling with my son in Latin America and made a point to meet my team in Brazil while we were in the neighborhood. It was during Thanksgiving, which isn't a holiday for them, but they made a big deal about it for us and involved the whole company in creating this Brazilian-style Thanksgiving dinner. We all went around the room and told each other some things we were thankful for, and it was the kind of special experience that I'll treasure forever.

When you're on Zoom you can connect minds, but when you're in person you're connecting hearts. You can find smart people in a lot of countries—India, the Philippines, Costa Rica, Argentina, Brazil—but smart people don't make a team. Team is about heart. Your outsourced people need to know that you really value and care about them, and you need to know that they're there for you, too.

It really doesn't take much to take things to the next level. In Latin America, they have a fascination with how much candy is available in the U.S., so one time I brought all these different types of candy. Every day, I'd come in with something different and it became the talk of the office.

If you read between the lines, you'll see that it wasn't just about giving them candy. It was more about the fact that I thought so highly of them that I would go through the effort of sharing a piece of my culture that they were interested in. And they did the same things. They'd bring in treats or delicacies from the area for me to try, and all of those actions contributed to the solid foundation of trust we were building.

It's amazing how much more dedicated people can be to a project when team members have bonded on a personal basis. One of the things that amazes me is how my teams have become little subcultures in their own companies. When they wear our T-shirts and talk about how great the relationship is, it really means something to the other people who work at our partner companies. Not only have we gotten more people interested in working for us, but we also have these little armies of engaged talent who advocate for our business within their companies because they're so proud of the sense of belonging they feel.

"In diversity there is beauty and there is strength."
—*Maya Angelou*

CHAPTER 7

AVOIDING THE BABEL EFFECT: TIPS FOR MANAGING GLOBAL TEAMS

The real work begins after you choose a partner and sign the contracts. That's when you'll want to get to know each other, establish team member roles, finalize your work plan, and set standards for communication, governance, and change management.

At this point the technical part should pretty much take care of itself, which can free you up to focus more on the people part of the success equation. As Jeff Shupack and Patrick Mee have already shared in their Guest Expert Spotlight sections (Chapters 1 and 2), this is where the team dynamics that can make or break your project will come into play. Everything rises or falls on leadership, and when that leadership is based on measurements, results, and compassion instead of gut feelings, hunches, and recency bias, it's more likely you'll have a unified team made up of happy, committed, and empowered people.

While a speedy integration of your internal and outsourced team members is always the goal, keep in mind that the onboarding and team integration process is ongoing. Every step of the way, you'll want to continuously evaluate your partner's ability to do quality work, communicate effectively, and adhere to timelines. And you'll want to make sure that the needs of your internal team members are being met so that the people around you will continue to support your outsourcing efforts.

Establishing the right relationship with a partner, maintaining it, and adapting it as needed will be your keys to successful multinational management and project completion.

It should go without saying that standing up an outsourcing project focused primarily on technical work items, and hoping for the best, leads to flawed outcomes and even epic failures. Too many business leaders fail to realize that management is even more important when blended and distributed teams are involved. Further, it's critical to make sure your practices and procedures are up to date and aligned for success.

Clear direction and team building at the onset of any outsourcing partner relationship provide the foundation for world-class execution by the blended team. If you don't know how to develop and manage an optimal working relationship with your chosen development partners—or if you don't see this as a critical step—then you don't deserve to get optimal results.

Twenty-five percent of outsourcing projects fail within two years, because of issues ranging from budget overruns and product delays to an underestimation of scope and a lack of cultural or work practice alignment. Some of these failures are catastrophic, while others simply rate as a bad experience that ends a working relationship with an outsourcing partner.

Your projects are far less likely to fall into the failure category if you nurture your outsourcing partner relationship from the beginning. Your early and continued investment in people and procedures will result in faster production, less rework, better quality, and higher performance from every team member.

Why Teams Fail

One of my favorite business books of all time is *The Five Dysfunctions of a Team* by Patrick Lencioni. Like a book I wrote with Steve Mezak in 2016 called *Outsource or Else!*, it uses a fable format to show how teams that are built without laying down a foundation of trust can quickly fall apart.

Throughout the fictionalized story of a company called DecisionTech, CEO Kathryn Peterson identifies what's preventing her team from thriving. The specific dysfunctions are:

1. **Absence of Trust**—Grows when team members aren't able to expose their vulnerabilities without fear of exploitation.
2. **Fear of Conflict**—Closes off communication and healthy debate.
3. **Lack of Commitment**—Creates ambiguity around what to do next and what goals the team should be shooting for.
4. **Avoidance of Accountability**—Leads to lower standards and inconsistencies.
5. **Inattention to Results**—Causes an "every-man-for-himself" mentality, which is the exact opposite of what a team should be.

While not all fables have happy endings, the one created by Lencioni does. The DecisionTech team overcomes its dysfunctions through a set of team dynamics that rely on trust, candor, commitment, and accountability.

In the story, trust is built by sharing personal stories, understanding personality profiles, and creating an environment where it's okay to take risks. Teams that cultivate this kind of vulnerability-based trust create a safe environment that empowers team members to share ideas, give and receive feedback, and collaborate effectively.

The second dysfunction, fearing conflict, is mastered by acknowledging its value and encouraging team members to engage in constructive debates, welcome feedback, and avoid back-channel politics and personal attacks. Teams that engage in healthy conflict can leverage differing perspectives and ideas to reach better decisions, leading to stronger commitment and successful outcomes.

Commitment is enhanced by establishing deadlines, clearly defining responsibilities, and agreeing to abide by decisions made after everyone has ample time to voice their opinions. Accountability is facilitated through regular progress reviews and open channels of communication.

Because fostering accountability leads to a greater willingness among team members to take ownership of individual and collective responsibilities, performance at DecisionTech went through the roof and further sharpened the now highly functional team's focus on shared objectives, innovation, and growth.

Syncing Your Teams for High Functionality

The principles outlined in *The Five Dysfunctions of a Team* work in real life as well as fiction. Not only do we try to follow Lencioni's ideas in our own organization, but we also use them as the foundation for special workshops we conduct when our clients start new outsourcing engagements.

Later in this chapter, I'll go into great detail about how we help clients and their outsourcing partners work as "One Team." But right now I just want to highlight some of the non-negotiables that make team alignment possible so you can keep them in your mind as you keep reading.

Essentially, all you really need to manage a multinational team effectively are shared expectations and a collaboration framework that people use. You can have everything organized and written down, and you can implement the best workflow efficiency tools available, but your in-house and outsourced people must all buy into the vision.

I'm all for comprehensive documentation, but only if it leads to a clear understanding of—and agreement over—goals, roles, accountability, approach, communication formats, decision-making, and other best practices. And I'm all for advanced collaboration tools, but only with proper training, continuous oversight, and support and participation from the top down.

Optimizing individual and team effectiveness, efficiency, and productivity is the job of any good manager. While the principles are simple, carrying them out is difficult even without multinational complexity thrown in. But heading off the risk of project breakdowns is definitely worth the effort, and if you follow this advice you'll be well on your way to achieving outsourcing and multinational management success.

Outsourcing Team Management Tips

Before I explain my team alignment methodology, I'd like to call your attention to the work of Michael F. Corbett, an outsourcing expert who founded the International Association of Outsourcing Professionals and currently serves as its chairman.

Back in 2004, Corbett wrote a great book called *The Outsourcing Revolution: Why It Makes Sense and How to Do It Right*. He understood how outsourcing was changing the role of managers and executives, moving them "away from functional or operational expertise and toward the integration skills that top managers have always needed," namely the ability "to think strategically, to make deals, to govern partnerships ... and to manage change."

- **Strategic Thinking**—Understanding when and how to outsource for competitive advantage
- **Deal Making**—Getting the right services from external partners and assuring their use by internal managers
- **Partnership Governing**—Effective oversight of outsourced relationships

- **Change Managing**—Overcoming resistance among in-house team members and other company employees

According to Corbett, outsourcing puts a greater focus on balancing competing interests and keeping everyone attentive to the task at hand. Adding to the difficulty is the need to adjust to the different work styles and sensibilities of people from different cultures and countries.

This effort is worth it, Corbett says, because as outsourcing matures in an organization the organization has the potential to radically transform. Corbett has documented the shift of many companies, including household names like Dell, Cisco, and Intel, which have "turned outsourcing from a supply chain mechanism into an innovation chain, delivering not new hardware, but new ways of doing business."

Corbett goes on to say that "because innovation is based on knowledge—whether information about employees, customers or operational systems—managing knowledge will be more important than ever. The challenge is to facilitate and encourage the sharing of knowledge across business structures and units. Risk management will also see profound change. Outsourcing makes organizations more interdependent, so risks that affect an outsourcing partner now also affect the domestic firm. Thus, U.S. firms must hold their foreign partners accountable for compliance with standards and regulations."

According to Corbett, about 2% of the value of a typical outsourcing contract is spent managing the vendor relationship. And the return on that investment can be immense if you manage your vendors—and internal team members—according to these principles:

1. Maintain strategic responsibility by putting a top executive in charge of the outsourcing relationship.
2. Create and promote multiple channels of communication between your company and your outsourcing partners.
3. Hold regular meetings to ensure progress and to catch any issues early before they become major problems.
4. Use digital communication and collaboration tools.

5. Define clear and consistent escalation and remediation processes.
6. Define and agree to the metrics that will define success, and continuously keep a scorecard to make sure your teams are progressing toward goals in a timely manner.
7. Motivate and reward achievement with incentives and hold team members accountable through fair and consistently applied penalties.
8. Make your vendor's employees feel like they're really part of your team.
9. Clearly define the ways in which both firms will address the need for change.
10. Honor the relationship with your outsourcing partner and treat it like the strategic asset it is.

Key Considerations for Aligning Teams

In Search of Perfect Team Alignment

Psychological researcher Bruce Tuckman's breakthrough research into group dynamics led to the *forming–storming–norming–performing* model of group development, which he first introduced in 1965. To paraphrase Tuckman, new teams form, storm, and norm as they learn how to perform together—in either beneficial or dysfunctional ways.

As I understand Tuckman's thinking, each stage in the team development process is fixed and inevitable. All team members come together, start to learn about each other, get into a normalized work routine, and then perform at a certain level.

If one stage of development goes awry, it'll impact the next stage—much like the story that was told in *The Five Dysfunctions of a Team*. So the goal, according to Tuckman, is to prevent dysfunction by optimizing each stage of development so that it leads into the next stage in a positive way.

Tuckman's ideas about the critical elements that lead to team success very much dovetail with Lencioni's advice: shared understanding, trust that allows for vulnerability, and being open to constructive conflict are foundational elements in both models of successful team dynamics.

One of the more interesting things that Tuckman discovered is that when things go well, the norming stage enables team members to tolerate, overlook, and put aside each other's quirks and idiosyncrasies in service to the larger goal. Sometimes team members get caught up in the idea that they have to love everything about each other in order to be successful, when in fact people can annoy each other and still be effective coworkers. In reality, all that's needed is acceptance and respect for projects to go well—likeability is a bonus.

If the first three stages of Tuckman's *forming–storming–norming–performing* model proceed the way they should, the sky's the limit when it comes to the performing part. When people understand and honor each other's roles and responsibilities, when they can use their knowledge and motivation—both independently and collaboratively—to achieve common goals, and when they can channel disagreement and dissent in appropriate ways, teams can perform at exceedingly high levels.

Making this happen requires excellent managers who put an emphasis on optimizing interpersonal relationships and clear communication at every stage of the team building process. If your team isn't aligned from the beginning, then it's less likely that it'll ever come together.

Success just isn't possible without the right upfront investment, so how do you do it? At Accelerance, we conduct three-day, professionally facilitated alignment workshops (preferably in person) to bring our clients and their outsourcing partners together at the beginning of their engagements. The goal is to learn what it takes to operate as "One Team."

It's important to note that these workshops aren't instructor-led training sessions that teach a "right way" to develop software. Instead, they're collaborative sessions where everyone involved in the software development process can make decisions about how to work and solve problems together. Because people will usually defend what they create, the workshops get projects off to a great start by building a solid team foundation for success.

You'll no doubt notice that the principles outlined in *The Five Dysfunctions of a Team*, as well as Tuckman's *forming–storming–norming–performing* model, come to life in the way we structure our alignment workshops. We've worked hard to develop a workshop agenda that's proven to get results, but as long as you cover all the bases you can set your own teams up for success in whatever way works for you.

For starters, use our workshop template as a guide for creating clear expectations around roles and responsibilities, collaboration tools, communication guidelines, and effective work styles, operations, processes, and methodologies.

Laying this groundwork will go a long way toward enhancing team dynamics, boosting morale, and ensuring that your blended team is effective, efficient, and productive right from the start. This will make multinational management much easier and help you strengthen areas that can strain a partnership if not worked out in advance. These areas include:

1. **Culture Mapping**—How will we manage a multicultural team?
    - Who are we?
    - Team and individual team styles
    - Work ethics and norms
    - Structural expectations
2. **Shared Project Vision**—What are we trying to achieve?
    - Engagement scope and goals
    - Milestones and plan
    - Measurements, KPIs, and reporting
3. **Team Roles**—Who will do what?
    - Definitions for each role
    - Individual and team assignments
4. **Clear Communications**—How can we interact most effectively?
    - Language proficiency assessment
    - Tools and use cases
    - Glossary of common terms (industry, product, software, project)
5. **Global Team Practices**—How will the blended team operate?
    - Meeting cadence, agenda, and facilitation
    - Scheduling across time zones
    - Common governance processes
6. **Methodologies & Tools**—What is the unified development approach?
    - Software development lifecycle
    - Agile development process and team protocols
    - Backlog grooming and systems

Breaking the Ice—Finding Out Who We Are

The first thing we do in our workshops is start to get to know each other. Not only does this break the ice before three intense days of meetings, but it also helps prevent the kind of "us versus them" mentality that can develop in teams that are set up with separate groups of in-house and outsourced people.

We simply go around the room and have each team member complete the following statements:

- My ideal vacation is ___________________.
- Once upon a time, I ___________________.
- The riskiest thing I ever did was ________________.
- The wildest thing I ever did (that I'll admit to) is _______________.

While it may seem kind of silly, these relatable statements do a lot to break down walls and create a sense of shared humanity. This will become the foundation of the shared vision we want everyone to have for the project.

Depending on what each person says, these ice breakers can help team members form bonds and connections with each other so they can start to strengthen their working relationships before they even get started. It's amazing when people from totally different cultures begin to realize that they can have similar interests and experiences, even when they're a world apart. Plus, if people answer honestly and are willing to be vulnerable, this exercise can go a long way toward building trust.

Getting to know your software development team, whether they're in Argentina, Poland, China, or anywhere else, is as critical as building positive connections in-house. Good working relationships can transcend national borders, and team members should feel no less valued living thousands of miles away than they would if they were in the same office.

Mapping Your Team's Ways of Being

One of the most interesting things we do at our workshops is talk about how people in different countries communicate, evaluate, lead, decide, trust, disagree, schedule, and persuade in different ways.

We use a powerful tool called the Culture Map, which was created by professor, author, and speaker Erin Meyer based on work she did at the Institut Européen d'Administration des Affaires (INSEAD), one of the world's leading international business schools. Coincidentally, Meyer's passion for effective multinational management is also rooted in her experience as a Peace Corps volunteer, and she's devoted her entire career to decoding the cross-cultural complexities that impact international business.

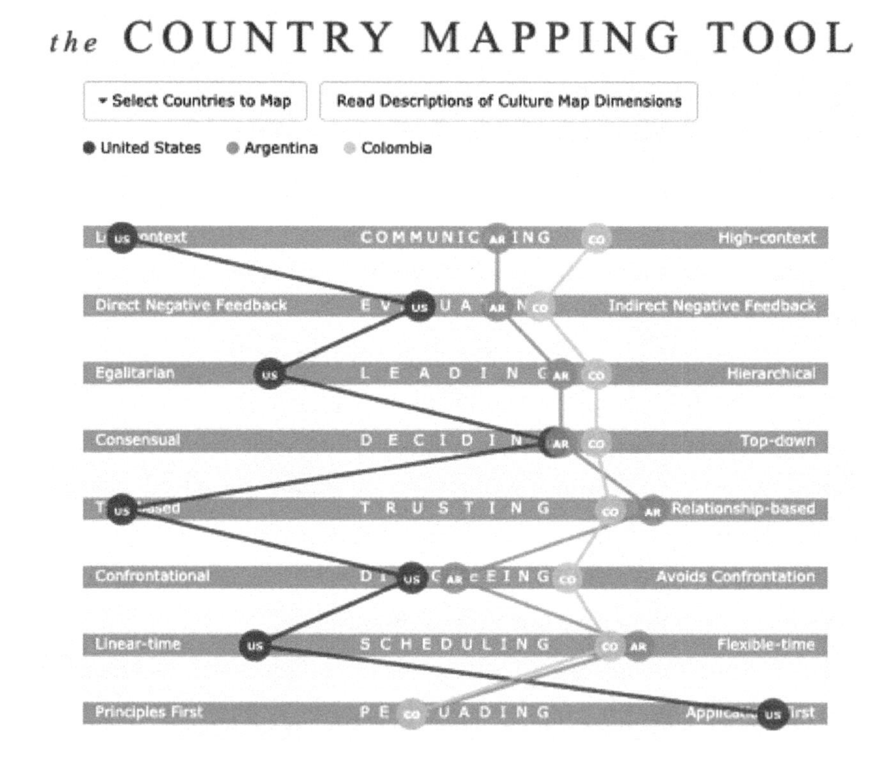

© Erin Meyer, The Culture Map

The Culture Map assesses workplace behavior in team member countries across eight key areas. The maps are very accurate, but keep in mind that individuals—within and across cultures—can vary considerably. Many people from India are quite punctual, for example, and many Dutch citizens are soft spoken. Someone from Brazil might be more schedule-obsessed than her compatriots, but still seem lax about timing and agendas to a Swiss colleague.

The point of this exercise is to gain insights into potential points of conflict and try to address them early. Here are some short descriptions of the different scales that the Culture Map analyzes:

Communicating
This scale measures the degree to which cultures are high- or low-context, a metric developed by anthropologist Edward Hall. In low-context cultures, such as the U.S., Germany, and the Netherlands, good communication is precise, simple, explicit, and clear. Messages are expressed and understood at face value. Repetition and written reinforcement are appreciated. In high-context cultures, such as Japan, India, and France, communication is sophisticated, nuanced, and layered. Messages are both spoken and read between the lines. Less is put in writing and more is left for verbal interpretation.

Evaluating
This scale measures a preference for frank versus diplomatic criticism. People from Spain, for example, are very direct when it comes to providing and receiving feedback, while people from Mexico prefer to give and receive negative comments in a gentler way.

Persuading
This scale measures a preference for inductive vs. deductive reasoning. Inductive describes reasoning that uses specific observations to make general conclusions, while deductive reasoning starts from a set of general premises and draws specific conclusions from them. While both forms of reasoning are useful, inductive reasoning is personal and experiential, while deductive reasoning is more fact-based. Individuals from Southern European and Germanic cultures tend to find deductive reasoning more persuasive, whereas Americans and British businesspeople typically prefer an inductive style.

Leading

This scale measures the degree of respect and deference shown to authority figures, placing people on a spectrum between egalitarian (e.g., U.S. and Israel) and hierarchical (e.g., China, Russia, France, and Japan). This metric is based on the concept of power distance—which social psychologist Geert Hofstede first researched via surveys of IBM managers around the world in the 1970s—and on the work of Professors Robert House and Mansour Javidan, which was published in *The Globe Study of 62 Societies*.

Deciding

This scale explores differences between building group agreement and relying on an individual (usually the boss) to make decisions. We assume that egalitarian cultures rely on consensus to make decisions, while the boss makes unilateral decisions in hierarchical cultures. This isn't always the case. The Japanese, for example, are strongly hierarchical and consensual. The Germans are more hierarchical than Americans, but they're also more likely to make decisions as a group.

Trusting

Here we balance cognitive trust (from the head) with affective trust (from the heart). In task-based cultures, like the U.S., Britain, and Germany, trust is built through work (we work well together, we like each other's work, we like each other—so I trust you). In relationship-based societies, like Brazil, Japan, and India, trust comes from personal, affective connection (we've laughed together, shared time relaxing together, gotten to know each other at a deep personal level—so I trust you).

Disagreeing

People from different cultures—and people in general—can have different ideas about the value of confrontation. People from countries like China, Japan, and India often frown on the public airing of disagreement, while people from the U.S., France, and the Netherlands are usually okay with spirited debates during meetings. This scale measures how people think open disagreement is likely to improve group dynamics or harm team relationships.

Scheduling

All businesses follow timetables. In some cultures, such as India, Brazil, and Italy, people often treat a schedule as more of a suggestion, while people in other cultures, like Switzerland, Germany, and the U.S., expect everyone on the team to stick to the agenda. This metric looks at how much value people place on being structured versus reactive. It's based on the "monochronic" and "polychronic" distinction that was formalized by anthropologist and cross-cultural researcher Edward Hall.

Scale descriptions adapted from content licensed through the Team Mapping Tool and © Erin Meyer, 2021.

After we talk about cultural differences in our workshops, we look at how individual team members are mapped across the same eight scales. Before the workshop, each team member receives a unique url they can visit to answer a few questions about themselves and generate a personalized report. When the team members get together, we share the results with everyone and see how the whole team fits together. We talk about potential points of conflict, and analyze where compromises might need to be made.

It's quite fascinating to discover the philosophy behind the different ways we try to communicate and influence people; to find out who operates from a practices first mindset and a principles first mindset; and to realize how much our cultural norms impact different approaches.

Tom Cooper, one of our consultants who leads many of our alignment workshops, told me that when he was in Ukraine one time he noticed a sign that said it was okay to turn right on red. It was a little thing, but it dawned on him that in that culture the default position is prohibition. A sign must tell you that it's okay to turn right on red, otherwise you can't do it.

For people living in that culture, signs like that reinforce the idea that they can't take action unless permission is given. Knowing that there's a cultural norm of pausing until permitted to move forward can help leaders think about how to communicate with the team, being careful to express that team members are expected to take initiative, take risks, and innovate. Perceptive leaders can watch for signs of risk taking and celebrate them to reinforce the team value of taking initiative and trying new things, even when not specifically directed to do so.

In another example, we had a team where the cultural norm was top-down decision making. In other words, decisions were typically made by the boss. We sometimes call that the highest paid person's opinion (HiPPO). Agile development, however, depends on team members being able to offer their insights and observations about plans and problem solving. On this team, we noted that when the project manager spoke, the team quickly fell in line with whatever he said. To overcome that social pressure, the team created a rule that said the project manager couldn't weigh in on an issue until everyone else had a chance to express their opinions. If the project manager went first everyone would agree with him, but the new rule allowed dissenting points of view to be expressed without violating a cultural norm.

These are the types of hidden differences that can have a profound impact on successful team dynamics if they're discovered and addressed. Managers need to see things through a cultural lens to understand what's really going on. When a team member from East Asia says that something will be "very difficult," a perceptive manager needs to be aware that it might really mean, "There's no way it's going to happen."

In one situation we had with a team in South America, the client wanted a particular software architect to attend meetings. The person often skipped these meetings, though, because he didn't think they added value to his role. This was insulting to the person paying the bills, who would have gotten value if the architect was in attendance. No one said anything but you could tell that the client was getting upset, so it took a leader who was carefully watching the dynamics to notice that the architect's lack of attendance was putting team performance at risk.

Learning each team member's instincts and blind spots before work commences can be incredibly valuable for making sure minor issues and irritations don't balloon into major problems. When disconnects occur, we can take a step back, realize that it's likely not because someone is acting with bad intent, and work together to address the issues.

Creating a Shared Project Vision

After we gain insights into the different cultural and individual work styles that make up the team, we align everyone on a shared vision that outlines the scope of the project and the goals that need to be achieved. Typically this is presented in writing, with ample opportunities for people to ask questions.

Key components of the presentation include a milestone-based project plan, with a discussion about contingencies if things go off track. We also discuss how success will be measured, including the specific KPIs we'll use to track performance.

And lastly, we talk about how progress will be reported. This discussion includes information about what reports will be generated, how often they'll be generated, and who will receive them.

Defining Roles and Responsibilities

The next step in our alignment workshops consists of explaining the roles and responsibilities of each team member so everyone knows who's going to be doing what. We literally present a list that includes each person's name, job title, and a description of their role. Because several people can have more than one role, and because different people can all have the same role, all those nuances are indicated on the list provided.

Establishing Communication Guidelines

Based on the insights gained from our culture mapping, shared vision, and roles and responsibilities discussions, we talk about ways the team can interact most effectively.

In this section of the workshop, we go through a thorough language proficiency assessment and present a glossary of industry, product, software, and other terms that will be frequently used throughout the project. This is particularly useful for members of blended teams, who may use different terminology based on their location and business experience. Starbucks, for example, serves drinks to customers. Chick-fil-A, however, serves beverages to guests. Both brands serve liquid refreshment to people, but each one uses different language. While these terms are often second nature to people working in the business, it's important to share these types of references with new team members and clarify what they mean.

Because Agile software development is more about philosophy than a rigid set of practices, one often finds lots of different opinions about the words being used by team members. For example:

- When you say "Agile" or "sprint," what do you mean exactly?
- When you say "QA," do you mean unit test, smoke test, acceptance test, regression testing, or automated testing?
- When is "done" done?

We can be incredibly confident in our definitions, but if someone else has a different interpretation it can lead to significant waste and rework. So many areas can go sideways that it's important to agree on the definitions of as many terms as possible to avoid confusion.

Most organizations put a lot more emphasis on completing tasks than orienting new team members. As a result, when someone joins a team they often struggle to gain the critical and often hidden tribal knowledge that allows them to successfully complete their work. Taking the time to agree on and document these terms and processes gives new team members a fast path to coming up to speed, and lets all team members operate together without guessing what someone else means.

Miscommunication slows teams down, and it's often these hidden inefficiencies that make corporate leaders ask, "Why does it take us so long to ship working code?" As part of the team alignment process, we create a living reference guide, either as a PDF or an online wiki that people can update regularly as needs arise.

In this part of the workshop, we also discuss what collaboration and messaging tools we'll be using. From email, texts, and Slack to reports, meetings, and task-based digital tools, we talk about the importance of each channel and how they can be optimized. The goal is to keep complexity to a minimum and have each team member agree on which information will be communicated in which channels.

Of course, no modern development project can be managed well without a ticketing system. But using a ticketing system alone leads to throwing items over the fence, often with scant or cryptic notes that can lead to the kind of "us vs. them" thinking that we strive to avoid as we operate as one team.

Because we've never been more electronically connected than we are today, we have system access almost anywhere and at any time. If a leader happens to look at an issue late on a Friday night and has an idea about next steps, how will he or she communicate that to the team? And if a message is sent off hours, what's the expectation for a response? What tools should be checked and how often?

An assigned team member may be enjoying family time when an alert pops up on their mobile phone. Without clarity around expectations, the team member may feel anxiety about whether to stay with the family or address the issue. Meanwhile, the leader, who was just checking something off the list that could be handled the following week, may be completely unaware of the stressful impact on the team member. Such misunderstandings can erode trust and accountability, so it's really important to work through things early on.

We've found it useful to set expectations for what qualifies as a standard priority communication and what qualifies as an urgent priority communication. If an immediate answer is needed, which tool should be used? Are we expecting team members to constantly monitor the IM tool, WhatsApp, or texting? During what hours (or time zones)?

When something is less urgent, should we expect to see that in email, the ticketing system, or in some other to-do list tool? For example, the team may agree to respond to standard messages about things like locating documents and group status updates within one business day, while aiming for an immediate response to more urgent requests.

Typical Communication Protocol

Purpose	Tool	Timeframe
Reporting bugs - feature requests - anything requiring the attention of develoment	Ticketing system	Meet at least weekly to discuss newly submitted tickets
Urgent quick question for a team member	MS Teams	Team to be available 9-5 M-F local time. Other availability is "best effort"
Project updates, scheduling calls or meetings	Email	Team members check 1x a day and respond within one business day
Updates on previously reported information	Ticketing system	Single "source of truth" when it comes to tracking specifics

As a final note about communication protocols, it's very important to be aware of silence. If any team members are chronically late to, or absent from, meetings they need to attend, if they ignore emails, texts, phone calls, and other requests, or if they communicate poorly and fail to ask good questions, these are early warning signs that your project may be in trouble. In these situations, you should definitely intervene and course correct as soon as possible.

Travel Tip: Face-to-Face Communication Is Important

If possible, bring as many people from your in-house team as you can to visit your outsourcing partners in their country every few months. This will go a long way toward keeping relationships open, authentic, and strong over the course of your engagement. When you're visiting, plan on spending about half your time working and the other half socializing and team building.

We can't expect other people to behave like us all the time, but we can get to know them and think collaboratively in certain ways. There's nothing like walking down the streets in Colombia, India, Poland, or any other country to get a sense of what reality is like for people on your team. When you see a government-built apartment complex that's a mile and a half long, for example, you recognize how challenging that is for artistry and can gain a deeper appreciation for the developers who live there and still do beautiful work.

Instituting Global Team Practices

While you can always change things if they're not working later, it's important to establish a baseline for how your blended team can operate efficiently and effectively. Next on the agenda at a typical alignment workshop is a discussion about how the blended team will operate.

For example, it's important to understand how often meetings will be scheduled, how they'll be documented, and how team members will accommodate time zone differences. All these seemingly minor issues are important to clarify—and agree on—early in the process so there aren't any big surprises when the real work begins. Other key considerations include:

- What standards do we need to set?
- How can we work to make sure that we're following them?

- When someone doesn't follow the process, how will we address it?
- What failure modes need to be modeled?
- What is the suggested end-to-end workflow?
- Who needs to be "in the loop" when certain issues are discussed?
- How can we involve all stakeholders and decision makers early and often?

The main point of this part of the workshop is to establish a common governance process that will monitor and guide your project to successful completion. Good governance keeps everyone accountable to the project plan—and to each other—and enables course correction if things go off track.

Our overarching goal is to create One Team, with a laser-like focus on the mission of "Together, we're learning to build great software for this company." Knowing that every day won't be a good day, we agree on what we would do in the best situations and agree to work collaboratively to solve the inevitable problems that come up.

Continuous support goes hand in hand with good governance, and the best team leaders help members of the team get comfortable with following the plan. While everyone can agree on the software development lifecycle, the meetings they'll have, and the decisions they'll make, they might need a little hand holding before they really start to do things well. That's to be expected, and it's another way to learn about each other and establish trust. You might need to conduct daily standup meetings for a certain period of time, or work with some individual team members more than others. Take the time you need to empower everyone to do the things they said they were going to do.

Two areas where teams get into trouble involve defining goals and deciding if those goals were achieved or not. Frequently, someone will come up with an idea for a feature and ask a developer to define requirements. The problem is that developers are notoriously terrible at defining requirements because they want to focus on creating clever and elegant technical solutions to problems. The nature of the business problem is not particularly interesting to the average developer.

You wouldn't ask a plumber to do your electrical work, would you? We want to avoid asking the wrong person to do the wrong job. If we agree that a developer shouldn't have to "fill in the gaps," we'll define rules about how we'll know when a piece of work is "developer ready." And, when a developer looks at an assignment and realizes it's not ready, they'll be empowered to push back and say, "I'm not sure what you're trying to do here." With shared agreement about rules and roles for how the team does things, you can avoid future problems and have a path and plan for when things don't go as intended.

Once your developers start receiving the tasks they're most suited for, your governance model should provide a way of measuring when those tasks are completed. We regularly spend time discussing when done is really done in our workshops. Engineers believe something's done when they figure out how they can write the algorithm. Project managers say it's done when code goes from development to test. QA says it's done when it passes the test. But your customers don't say it's done until it works for them—in production!

When creating your governance system, make sure it covers the following categories:

Ongoing Assessments

- How much work did we estimate we could complete?
- How much did we complete?
- What lessons did we learn about planning and execution as we did this work?

Documentation

- What is our minimum standard?
- What must a developer do to say they've documented a user story or feature?
- What does DevOps or operations need to run the software?

- What does product management need to have in place for customers to use the software?

Team Operations

- Are we having the meetings needed to follow our process?
- Are the right team members in attendance?
- Are team members contributing what's expected?
- Are we meeting the professional development needs of our team members?
- How can we maintain morale and engagement?
- Are we addressing team member performance issues quickly and effectively?

Process Optimization

- How can we learn to work even more efficiently?
- What process improvements can we make as a team?

Program Plans

- Is the software development effort addressing specific business needs?
- How will we measure progress toward overall goals?
- How will we course correct?
- Is there a need to adjust based on market changes or lessons learned during the development process?

Issues Management

- When issues arise around contract terms, team member performance, or client responsibilities, when, where, and with whom will we clear the air and gain alignment?

Use Project Metrics for Data-Driven Decision Making

The last part of our alignment workshops focuses on data-driven decision making. Because numbers don't lie, you and your outsourcing partners must establish a clear set of project metrics for tracking and reporting progress throughout the engagement. Some considerations include:

- How will you measure individual success?
- How will you measure team success?
- How will you measure project success?
- What are your major milestones?

Having key performance indicators (KPIs) in place won't guarantee the absence of problems, but it will certainly help identify issues that need to be addressed and hold people accountable for their actions.

Capturing and analyzing KPIs in real or near real time not only shows how the actual project is proceeding according to plan, but can also provide detailed team member comparisons and help your blended team refine its ability to estimate time, cost, and human resource requirements.

The biggest disconnects typically occur when metrics aren't measurable, or when a leader relies on gut feel or experience instead of data. When you're thinking about metrics, consider how you'll know that things are working. Sometimes this is quantitative—"We'll have 5,000 transactions a month through the system, up from 2,000 today"—and other times it's qualitative—"In the next six months, we'll establish a pattern of shipping working code to production." The clearer you can be about the exact problems you're trying to solve, the more likely everyone will be on the same page about progress or lack of it.

One trap we see teams fall into is making incremental progress on some items but still not having complete features or upgrades ready to be shipped. It's far better to finish 100% of five features than it is to finish 80% of 10 features. Finish the tasks at hand, then go back and evaluate the ideas you had during the process that began with, "Wouldn't it be cool if…"

Revisiting *The 7 Habits*: Character Traits of Good Managers

All the way back in 1989, even before I joined the Peace Corps, Stephen R. Covey published his groundbreaking book on personal development and leadership, *The 7 Habits of Highly Effective People*. The book has definitely stood the test of time, selling more than 40 million copies in

Outsourcing Success Story: Blended Team as High-Performing Product Factory

With more than 40 offices in 20+ states, a leading management company leverages automated accounting systems, advanced technology, and a team of talented experts to help homeowner and condominium associations across the U.S. lower costs, protect property values, and improve the quality of life for residents.

The company attributes a large part of its success to the sophistication of its technology. As a result, it invests in the continuous improvement of digital and automated tools that help real estate developers and property managers effectively and efficiently serve their communities.

In an effort to become a high-performing product factory, the firm's executives saw an opportunity to outsource some of their software development work. At the time, the company was preparing for a major platform build that required the IT team to expand its capacity and enhance internal processes and procedures for staffing, onboarding, and managing larger-scale subgroups.

After we helped project leaders find a team in Argentina that met their exact business requirements and specialized technical skills, we helped them onboard and integrate their new developers, learn how to effectively manage a blended, international team, and improve their project management capabilities.

With the outsourced team in place, including QA engineers, business analysts, a project manager, full-stack developers, designers, and HTML developers, the schedules of six internal people were opened up for higher-order problem solving. This meant that the software being developed could focus on the highest-value business problems at hand.

40 languages and consistently ranking high on lists of the most influential business management books of all time. Most recently Sean Covey, Stephen Covey's son, contributed some key takeaways for the modern age in a special 30th Anniversary edition of the book, which has become a bestseller in its own right.

At my company, Accelerance, we do our best to follow the habits described in the book every day. They've inspired me since I read the original book back in the 1980s, and I've seen the timeless principles advance the careers of hundreds of colleagues over the years. What I've really noticed in all this time is how developing those habits can make people better managers and leaders, especially when blended international teams are involved.

The collection of habits knows no boundaries, which is why the book has been a bestseller in more than 40 countries, including many of those where outsourcing thrives today. I encourage you to get a copy of the book—I recommend the 30th Anniversary edition because it's been updated for the digital age—and begin cultivating the seven habits in your daily business and personal life.

Here's a brief summary of the habits and how they apply to multinational management:

1. **Be Proactive**
   Take responsibility for your actions, choices, and attitudes, and focus on what you can control rather than blaming others or reacting to external circumstances. Outsourcing itself can be used as a proactive strategy that drives growth and builds business resilience, so if you're even considering multinational management you're already developing this habit. Once you begin to manage geographically distributed teams, the additional variables and complexity will show you just how easy it is to be reactive. But if you put yourself in charge proactively, you'll establish the framework required to get things done. The most important things we've discussed in this book—establishing your readiness for outsourcing, properly vetting potential partners,

and aligning your blended team from the start—are all examples of this first habit in action.

2. **Begin with the End in Mind**
   The second habit embodies what we spend the most time on in our alignment workshops: establishing a shared vision and goals, assigning specific roles and responsibilities, and determining what success will look like when the team completes its important work. Knowing what you want to achieve makes it easier to develop a plan for getting there. And having a plan will help you stay focused and motivated, even when you hit unexpected twists and turns that force you to make modifications.

3. **Put First Things First**
   The third habit is about prioritizing tasks and activities, which is essential when working according to the principles of the Agile methodology in software development. Teams implement the most important user stories first, the features that are the most valuable to customers are tested the most, and standups establish priorities for each day.

4. **Think Win-Win**
   The fourth habit is about seeking mutually beneficial solutions and collaborations, and striving for a mindset of cooperation and shared success. This is especially important when working with people from different cultures who may have different values and priorities. It may not be quite as obvious, but managers of international teams can still find ways in which everyone can win.

5. **Seek First to Understand, Then to Be Understood**
   The fifth habit is critical for multinational management success because cultural differences can often lead to misunderstanding. When working with people from other cultures, you need to allow extra time to clarify communication and make sure you're on the same page. And the more patient and respectful you can be as a manager when it comes to these types of things, the more effective you'll be-

come. What's more, in addition to leading to greater understanding, this habit also helps to build trust and rapport, making communication and collaboration easier as you go along.

6. **Synergize**

   The sixth habit is about creating something that's greater than the sum of its parts. While this should be the goal of any team, the results can be even more powerful when you bring people together with different approaches to software problems and perspectives on life. By embracing diversity, the collaborative work you and your multinational team do will be more likely to create innovative solutions and achieve greater results.

7. **Sharpen the Saw**

   The seventh habit is about taking care of yourself physically, mentally, emotionally, and spiritually so you can be your best self. Immersing yourself in a totally different culture is a great way to do this. Falling in love with the culture of your outsourcing partners—and enthusiastically sharing your culture with them—is a perfect way to enrich your life and keep your saw as sharp as it can be.

GUEST EXPERT SPOTLIGHT

OLIVIER POULARD

Olivier Poulard is currently Head of Software Engineering & Delivery with Enlace Health. His largest outsourcing project involved a total of 800 people, with 600 developers offshore across five locations in India, Ukraine, and Russia. The "internal" team was also distributed among offices in England, Ireland, and the U.S.

Effective Outsourcing is About People, Not Contracts

Motivate your teams by communicating what's really in it for them.

In my experience, effective software development outsourcing is a mindset issue more than anything else. Everyone involved, whether in-house or offshore, needs to know what's in it for them before they'll really commit to the project—and to working well together.

While compensation is important, most people are looking for additional incentives and opportunities that they couldn't get anywhere else.

Internal team members, for example, might be motivated by the chance to focus on higher-level business and architecture decisions, while the offshore team handles the day-to-day coding effort. By becoming business and technical subject matter experts, your internal team members effectively get promoted as higher-level engineers and can build new, highly marketable skills.

You can also explain to your internal team members that bringing in offshore talent is the only way to ensure rapid scalability, while reassuring them that when the project is done the internal team will stay and the offshore team will be gone.

Experience with an offshore team can also expand your in-house people's horizons, by exposing them to new technologies and giving those willing to travel a chance to experience a new culture firsthand.

The same holds true for your outsourced teams. What's in it for them could include similar resume expanders, like the chance to work on something that's never been done before, or the opportunity to visit—or even transfer to—a different country for a time. When I was working in London, we would often have people from our teams in India work on-site with us for a year or more.

When you're selecting an outsourcing partner, it's important to make cultural alignment the key consideration. If your partner is excited about the opportunities that exist beyond getting compensated for their work—if they can really see what's in it for them and the talent they deliver to your project—then your offshore team is much more likely to feel like a real part of YOUR team.

In my largest outsourcing project, we benefited greatly from the fact that all our partners in India, Ukraine, and Russia were willing to overlook their competitive nature and genuinely collaborate with each other.

When you can create this same mindset in your in-house and outsourced people, you effectively create what I call a "oneshore" team of committed developers who respect each other, enjoy working together, and understand that the success of your project is very much in their own self-interest.

"No man is an island entire of itself; every man is a piece of the continent, a part of the main."
—John Donne

CHAPTER 8

TALENT SHORTAGE OR SURPLUS? STAYING RELEVANT WITH THE RISE OF AI

The tremendous demand for software and related services has led to a shortage of software architects, developers, engineers, machine learning experts, data scientists, data analysts, cybersecurity professionals, and related roles in recent years.

With more than 25 million active software developers worldwide, it's hard to believe there could be a talent shortage, but there is. Not only are colleges and universities not graduating people fast enough, the slow pace of change at these institutions results in fewer people with the skills most companies want today. This requires additional training and certifications to get people up to speed.

Add to this the fact that software development can be a short-lived career for many individuals. Most developers are under age 35, and the tech industry is notorious for its high resignation rate due to burnout.

The scarcity of technical skills needed to fully drive digital transformation efforts poses a threat to businesses across all sectors and industries. It can take months to fill an open software engineering position, and competition pushes rates so high that many companies can't afford domestic talent.

As we've already discussed, looking for individuals and teams outside a company's home country has been—and continues to be—a valuable strategy for expanding the talent pool and filling open positions more quickly. But as more companies look for trusted outsourcing partners and work to expand their multinational management capabilities, the global software development market will no doubt become more competitive.

Will AI End Software Development?

Many people are hopeful that artificial intelligence (AI) will solve the technology talent shortage by automating certain development and engineering tasks. Some people are so confident that machines will take over that they're worried AI will ultimately make human software developers and engineers obsolete. We're in a transitory time for sure, and it's anybody's guess as to how everything will shake out.

I'm very interested to see what happens, and in the short term I'm excited about the productivity gains that can result when human practitioners are assisted by intelligent agents or copilots.

In a very short amount of time, AI has already had a major impact on the software development industry. Algorithms can almost instantly analyze large code repositories, understand patterns, and generate new code, saving developers time and effort by automating repetitive and mundane tasks.

AI has also improved the software testing process, automatically detecting and fixing bugs, optimizing performance, and ensuring compatibility across platforms.

Furthermore, AI has revolutionized customer support and service through the development of intelligent chatbots and virtual assistants that can interact with users, answer questions, and perform tasks like scheduling appointments and placing orders.

As AI technology advances, we can expect more sophisticated automated code generation tools, further improving the speed and efficiency of software development. AI will also play a crucial role in enhancing software security, as it can identify and predict potential vulnerabilities, helping developers build more robust and secure applications.

With the rise of connected devices, AI will also be vital in managing and analyzing the massive amounts of data generated by the Internet of Things (IoT). AI algorithms can extract meaningful insights from IoT data, enabling developers to build smarter and more efficient software systems.

As AI continues to evolve and integrate with current software development practices, we can expect further advancements in productivity, reliability, and innovation. Guided by experts, AI-powered copilots have the potential to enable a single developer or engineer to do the work of multiple people, effectively filling some of the currently open software development and engineering positions themselves. Using machines as tools, human developers and engineers will be faster and more productive, and they'll provide valuable feedback that will continuously improve the way human beings and machines work together.

The evolution of AI should relieve at least part of the massive talent shortage we've been experiencing for years in the software development industry. It will also likely create new opportunities for human beings and new ways of working that we can't even comprehend right now.

Humans will be freed up to focus on the more complex and creative aspects of software development, such as designing innovative solutions that address real-world problems, understanding user requirements, and collaborating with stakeholders. Human developers possess the ability to think critically, apply logical reasoning, and adapt to changing circumstances, which are critical components in software development.

As AI becomes more proficient at software development itself, human developers will also likely shift toward roles that involve overseeing AI systems, ensuring ethical practices, and making high-level decisions. They may also involve themselves in areas where AI may still need guidance and that require deep domain knowledge, such as system architecture, data analysis, and algorithm design.

Future software developers will need to become experts at prompting AI tools. This will require a deep knowledge of AI capabilities, problem formulation, data selection, training strategies, evaluation techniques, bias mitigation, and continuous learning.

The developers with the best chance for success will exhibit a combination of technical skills and domain expertise, along with a strong understanding of ethical considerations. The way I see it, the software developer of the future will likely need to be adept at the following seven skills:

1. **Understanding AI Capabilities**
   Developers will need to have a deep understanding of the functionalities, limitations, and potential biases of AI tools. This knowledge will help them identify the appropriate tasks and use cases where AI can be effectively employed.

2. **Defining Problem Statements**
   Developers will need to be skilled at formulating clear and well-defined problem statements and prompts for AI tools. This involves breaking down complex problems into smaller, manageable tasks that can be solved using AI.

3. **Choosing Appropriate Data**
   Developers will need to select and prepare the right datasets to train AI models. This involves identifying relevant data that reflects the real-world scenarios where the AI is meant to work.

4. **Crafting Training Strategies**
   Developers will need to design and implement effective training strategies for AI models. This involves choosing appropriate algorithms, fine-tuning hyperparameters, and using techniques like data augmentation and transfer learning to improve the model's performance.

5. **Evaluating and Interpreting AI Output**
   Developers will need to validate and test AI models to ensure their reliability and accuracy and interpret results in the context of the problems being tackled.

6. **Addressing Biases and Ethical Concerns**
   Developers will need to be proactive in identifying and addressing biases to ensure that the AI tools they're using are fair, unbiased, and inclusive.

7. **Continuous Learning and Adaptation**
   Developers will need to stay up to date with the latest advancements in AI, to effectively prompt and utilize AI tools in their work.

A Flow of Information and Creativity

While we don't exactly know what the AI disruption in software development is going to look like, I think we can safely assume that the individual productivity of developers and engineers will increase dramatically in the short term. And at some point in the future, the role of developers and engineers may be defined in terms of how they interact with AI copilots.

Troy Hiltbrand, who you met in an earlier Guest Expert Spotlight (Chapter 6), asserts that the software development industry must start to figure out how to create, foster, and manage creative minds versus more code monkeys. He envisions a future flow of information and creativity, in which creative people define the use cases and get prompts into the right format, so that our AI tools can do the heavy lifting of creating the necessary code.

All of this will have an impact on the way clients and outsourcing partners work together. "How do your partners in Colombia, Brazil, India, the Philippines, and other countries become a conduit?" he asked rhetorically during a conversation we had recently. "Are they the ones that will manage prompt building while the client focuses more on business decisions? And how do you get all that into requirements? I do think that the business analysis aspect is going to be critical going forward."

Troy can even imagine a future where developers in the U.S. are replaced by expert business analysts, who can pull out requirements so they can be leveraged by prompt engineers located in other markets.

My friend Guillermo Kopp, who you'll meet in a future Guest Expert Spotlight (Chapter 9), told me recently that we're still living in the Bronze Age when it comes to AI, and that the inconceivable innovations that will occur in the generations ahead will create new sets of incredible competencies that will all need to be managed effectively.

Time will tell what clients do with the increased capacity for innovation. Assuming we're at 1x innovation today, companies have an important decision to make: Achieve the same level with one third of the people, or go to 3x innovation with the same number of people.

While it may require a lot of courage in some cases, I do believe that the best companies will take the opportunity to increase their innovation capacity instead of simply cutting costs to stay where they are.

GUEST EXPERT SPOTLIGHT

RICH MIRONOV

A seasoned tech executive and serial entrepreneur, Rich Mironov has been the 'product guy' at six different startups. He's a relentless blogger, speaker, teacher, and mentor on software strategy, product management, and aligning "what we can build" with "what markets will pay for." He wrote "The Art of Product Management" and is a voice for the scrappy entrepreneur in all of us.

I'm Not Worried about the Robots

While machines can be useful tools, we still need people who have empathy for users.

I really believe that people are both overestimating and underestimating the impact of AI today. Just as we've done with other technologies in the past, we're overestimating the impact in the short term, while underestimating it in the long term.

After the initial hype over ChatGPT, people started getting burned by information that was wrong or made up in many cases. So now we're frustrated, because if you're doing anything serious you have to be deeply suspect of the data and know enough about what you're doing to throw away the bad stuff.

While the danger of bad data has put a damper on things now, I expect that we'll figure out how to make AI work much better in the next few years. And, over the course of 10 to 20 years, AI will probably become the fundamental thing nobody can live without—just like the iPhone and Amazon.

When I was in school in the 1970s, I had some experience with a program called ELIZA, which could take a sentence and flip it around into a question. Our computer science professors put someone at the end of a chatbot and told the subject that they were connected to a human psychiatrist.

If a subject said, "I'm feeling lousy today," ELIZA would respond with, "Why are you feeling lousy today?" If the subject came back with, "I don't have any friends," ELIZA would say something like, "Tell me more about why you don't have any friends." On and on it would go, and people would start to think they were talking to a real psychiatrist. And then—just for fun and at random—ELIZA would say something like, "You haven't mentioned your mother."

Did this "AI" have any knowledge of anything? No, it was just a sentence reformatter. And as far as we've come with chatbots in the last 50 years, they're still not perfect. We still have people in the back chasing down all the errors and special cases.

It's a very difficult undertaking to get AI right, but we're putting a lot of brain power into the effort and are learning a lot by failing. One of the problems we're seeing with automation is that people get lazy. A few years ago, a couple of the big banks tried to automate the mortgage approval process using historical data. They fed everything into a machine learning model that could make a decision in two seconds that would take hours—or even days—for a person to make. One tiny problem was that all the historic redlining biases were picked up by the algorithm. People had to go back in, fix the models, and really think about what they were doing.

Another problem is that whenever we automate anything we stop paying attention to it. So I want to automate things that don't need much attention to begin with, and I want to attach alarms or alerts to them when they veer off course. We need some psychological schemes that force ourselves to check on our systems and data to make sure they're still doing what we thought they were going to do.

That's the nature of automation: We automate something, and then we don't see it anymore. As long as it doesn't get us into trouble, we're fine. AI gets off the rails sometimes and we don't notice.

That being said, I think AI tools are great for use cases where you can get 95% of the work done accurately in a nanosecond, so all you have to do is validate and edit the 5% that's erroneous. But that still requires knowing what's bad and what's good, especially when the stakes are high.

If we're writing thank you and apology letters to consumers who've used our low-priced product a few times, then I think it's okay to use a large language model to generate those communications. What's the harm? I still want somebody to look at them before they go out, but the AI isn't deeply involved in the conversation or making judgments. It's just taking notes and organizing them in a way that can be useful. And if it can eliminate busy work, then it's a valuable tool. But right now, that's all it is or can be—a tool.

I think all managers have an obligation to have an honest discussion with their teams about the parts of work they do that could be automated: Which parts of what you're doing all week can we give to a robot? If the answer is all of it, well, then you're fired, right? But I don't think that's the case yet. In these early stages, we need to measure our willingness to let robots handle certain mundane things, like notetaking and calendars. Is an executive willing to let AI write a talk he's giving to the customer forum next week? Probably not. But he might use it to get some ideas.

I think it's important to look at every instance of AI use as an experiment and take an Agile approach to it. For the next two weeks, let's all try pushing our calendar requests through the machine and then we can vote on whether we think it was better or worse. Was the time savings worth all the corrections and oversights?

My main point here is that if you understand what a tool does and how it works, you're going to be better at it. Take the time to understand what AI really does, instead of just being wowed and hypnotized by it. It's an easy trap to fall into because the people marketing these tools are only showing you the handful of examples that are really cool. What we don't see are the 800 previous iterations that were stupid and thrown away.

I'm a firm believer in things that AI can't do, and noticing subtleties is a big one. When we interview customers in the discovery or validation phase, we use open-ended questions to learn what they care about and we look for problems we haven't thought of before. What we're trying to do is figure out what's true in the world and talk to a bunch of folks about what they want and what they might pay for.

In those calls, I insist that we have what the renowned business thought leader Teresa Torres would call a trio. We need a product person, a designer, and an engineer on those calls in real time, not reading transcripts later on. We might have to mute the developers because they'll either say, "That's really easy, I'll have it for you on Friday" or "That's a stupid idea...Let me explain why you're stupid," but other than that I really want that trio of people to hear—in real time—what real people are saying about their real needs.

Designers, developers, and product managers all have different ears and hear different things, so they're going to ask different questions in those interviews. And the value of being in real time means that you can capture the magic that happens when somebody hears something that triggers a thought. If the engineer hears something that smells of scalability or security issues, then I want them to drop the follow-on question in a private chat to the person leading the interview to get more context and substance.

To be perfectly honest, the most important thing I've noticed in my years of working on software is that there's no substitute for having real empathy for human end users. My developers don't really care about what I tell them, what's written down, or what's in the ticket. But when my development team hears from users that they can't do their work because of the way the two- or three-factor authentication is set up, they're going to fix it come hell or high water.

I can tell my team that, and it has no emotional resonance. It's just a thing on a list. But when somebody who's real—somebody who's paid us or whose boss has paid us to use the B2B banking software we built—says they're going to get fired because we set up multi-factor authentication in a way that doesn't work for their cellular provider in Asia, it hits home.

What I see over and over again is that developers will stay up all night because they love our users and they're embarrassed when things don't work. It's a very human characteristic, not a machine attribute. So, I know that if I plug my designers and developers into what real people say about real things I can get 30% better work out of them and that's a big deal.

I'm not worried about the robots right now because building systems is hard intellectual work that requires real user input, nuanced human interactions, strategic thinking, and empathy. I'm all for using supervised machines to help get us part of the way there, but until they become human they'll simply remain tools that can help humans do important work. Have I asked you about your mother?

"There is no such thing as a self-made man. You will reach your goals only with the help of others."
—*George Shinn*

CHAPTER 9

WHAT'S ALL THE HYPE ABOUT HYPERSPECIALIZATION?

Automation through artificial intelligence—and to some extent the low code/no code capabilities that provide simple drag and drop solutions for creating applications—is making it possible for more people in more organizations to take care of some of the smaller software development tasks. This gives the core development team more room to focus on more important issues, and it also frees up some resources for outsourcing complex and specialized technology work to experts.

While companies are still asking how to get faster, leaner, and more digital, a new question of how to compete from a capabilities and talent perspective is shining a light on the skills businesses need. Demand for innovative and emerging technologies is rising, with key priorities falling in the following categories:

- Machine learning
- Natural language processing
- Cloud computing
- Robotic process automation (RPA)
- Data science/analytics
- Internet of Things (IoT)
- DevOps
- Cybersecurity

Spending on these specialized technologies has also been increasing across the United States and Europe, as companies look for ways to gain a competitive advantage.

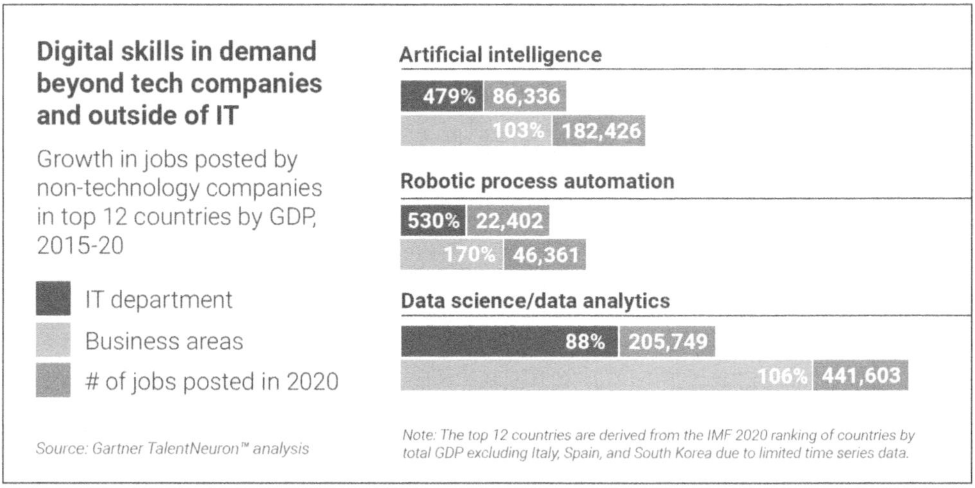

"Those with well-defined digital strategies and highly regarded IT departments already allocate less than half of their budgets (47%) to business operations and 26% to innovation," said a Deloitte Consulting report from 2021. "In the next three to five years, they plan to further reduce the operations allocation to a third of their annual budget while increasing innovation funding to 38%."

The demand for specialized technology expertise is increasing at businesses in all industries, not just technology companies. And we're noticing increased interest across the enterprise, not just in IT departments. As you can see in the chart on the previous page, business areas outside of IT showed the biggest growth in specialized technology job postings in recent years and the trend is showing no signs of slowing down.

In our current era of hyperspecialization, this is the winning strategy: Identify the technologies that will let you stand out and seek the best expertise to help you realize your vision.

I don't want to overstate this, and you should know that the majority of software development work still relies on core, well-understood technologies, but emerging and specialized technologies are important topics of conversation I have with clients every day. Innovation is becoming a top priority for IT leaders, and they're asking me how they can find people with skills in advanced, hyperspecialized technologies, platforms, and programming languages that are critical to cutting-edge projects.

The biggest problem right now is that the technical skills required to develop and maintain these technologies are in short supply. To get an understanding of the gap between the most common programming languages and the ones that are most in demand, just look at the chart on the next page. The most used programming languages on the left are generally easy to find and are relatively inexpensive, while the specialized programming languages on the right are rare and command the highest prices.

The same is true for databases, network development frameworks, and other areas of expertise: technologies that are commonly used are getting cheaper, while the exciting new technologies are getting more expensive as demand grows.

With high rates tied to scarcity, even if you have the money to pay for specialized skills you might not be able to get on anyone's schedule right away. According to the 2021 Harvey Nash Group Digital Leadership Report, more than 67% of IT leaders say that a lack of specialized talent is preventing them from keeping pace with digital change and innovation. For the last few years, hundreds of thousands of cybersecurity-related positions have been open in the U.S., and the same can be said for other disciplines.

Programming Languages

Most Used	Top Paying
JavaScript	Clojure
HTML/CSS	F#
Python	Elixir
SQL	Erlang
TypeScript	Perl
Java	Ruby
Bash/Shell	Scala
C#	Rust
C++	Go
PHP	LISP

Upskilling internal teams to leverage new technologies is costly and time-consuming, so the only practical option for most companies is to find outsourced talent to meet the demand. This can have the added benefit of letting companies just pay for what they need, as specialized talent is only required on a short-term basis in many cases.

For example, you may need a cloud architect to help you migrate your on-premises systems and support the design of new cloud-based applications. Do you hire someone full-time even though you don't need those skills every day? Could you contract with a more experienced cloud architect on a part-time basis for the same amount of money you could afford to pay a more junior person full-time? The same principles apply for other skills you might only need occasionally, such as deploying IoT devices, building machine learning models, and creating blockchain-based applications.

In many ways, hyperspecialization is changing the nature of software development by carving up projects into smaller components that require domain experts at different stages. Development projects need all the software engineers, designers, coders, and testers they've always needed, but they also require skilled experts in embedded systems, data science, machine learning, cybersecurity, and other capabilities to come in on an ad hoc basis.

To fill the gaps, most of the outsourcing partners we match with clients are increasing the depth and breadth of their areas of specialization. They're investing time and money to recruit developers with specialized expertise, train their own developers in new and emerging technologies, and keep their developers up to date as the technologies evolve.

The areas that are seeing the most activity these days are fairly predictable. Any technology associated with cloud-orientated services is receiving huge attention, along with quality assurance automation, DevOps, robotic process automation, and AI.

Accelerance client John Nelson, SVP of Engineering at Single Digits, an Internet service provider for property owners, has witnessed the evolution of hyperspecialization over the past decade. When he started at the company in 2012, the team was small and generalized, building an entire application with Java Enterprise. Later, John and his team started to modernize their application and embraced the cloud-native architecture of AWS.

Today, John leads ten teams of AWS platform engineers, each with a different specialty from reporting and analytics to data warehousing and mining. In addition to hiring more people in-house, John's also using more contract and offshore partners to find the skills he doesn't have locally. Recently, he's talked to various partners about having a bench of talent at the ready as the company's needs continue to evolve.

*****

If you're lucky enough to find the specialists you need, their knowledge can help you drive the development of new and innovative solutions that push the boundaries of what's possible. They can also give your existing team members a chance to learn about something new by collaborating with experts in emerging technologies. In many cases I've seen, the blending of an existing team with a few specialists has created exciting synergies that have led to new ideas and better-than-expected outcomes.

The key is finding the right balance between people who have specialized skills and those who can work across multiple technologies and integrate different systems.

Core backend financial, e-commerce, and operational systems continue to require the efforts of large teams of developers skilled in everything from C++ and .NET to Java and Ruby on Rails, but the move to cloud platforms, the rise of software as a service, and the impact of emerging technologies have created a demand for more complex software requirements.

Software architecture is evolving to be "hyperplexed, by which we mean that they will have to support many widely distributed software applications, several different types of devices, and new user experiences and interfaces," according to a recent Boston Consulting Group (BCG) report.

BCG asserts that the growing use of AI, robotics, AR/VR, IoT, and 5G networks is creating a pressing need for the next generation of software architectures. "On the one hand, the new technologies have developed platforms and tools that will help solve difficult problems cheaper and faster than ever before," the BCG report says. "On the other hand, they have greatly increased the complexity of software architectures, forcing companies to rethink how they develop software."

Consider the skills needed to support blockchain technology development. Blockchain developers can utilize well-established languages like Java, Python, and C++ that boast large-scale libraries, long community support history, and enormous installed user bases, but new languages are emerging to address hyper-targeted programming needs.

Solidity, for example, is a top blockchain coding option because of its proficiency in developing decentralized applications (dApps) and its contract orientation. GoLang is a compiled multi-threaded programming language that allows different processes to run simultaneously across multiple blockchain parts, fueling its popularity in the non-fungible token (NFT) marketplace.

As complexity continues to increase, and as humans continue to be attracted to the next big thing, companies will have to fill a growing need for specialized skills that will be difficult to procure, while at the same time maintaining investments in legacy technologies.

While this type of balancing act isn't easy, companies that have an ability to manage multinational teams and have had successful relationships with outsourcing partners will be in the best position to succeed.

GUEST EXPERT SPOTLIGHT

GUILLERMO KOPP

Currently CEO of GUAU Corporation—a company he co-founded in 2010 to help financial services executives tap emerging technologies and formulate strategic roadmaps—Guillermo Kopp spent his 16-year international staff career at Citigroup. A tenacious thought leader, he has domain expertise in risk management, payments, operational excellence, customer experience, complex program management, and technology leadership.

The Business Case for Values-Based Innovation

To get the full benefits of hyperspecialization, a cultural response is needed.

Technological hyperspecialization continues to create fantastic opportunities for global businesses. New platforms give creative people opportunities to explore, and, as innovations get rolled up into the global economic ecosystem, new itches to innovate arise that need to be satisfied.

It only takes a motivated person or team of people to get deep into a technology and suddenly strike gold with a new approach or use case. The defining technologies of today are generative AI, robotics, and quantum computing, and we're only scratching the surface of what they can do to resolve a completely different breed of challenges related to everything from financial services to cybersecurity.

As product cycles become shorter, and as technological disciplines combine with each other in exciting new ways, we'll see specialists and niche companies connect new value propositions with marketplace needs. One product will immediately lead to something better, along with a continued need for new development competencies.

The key question is this: How can we balance innovation with society's ability to accept it? A book called *The Island*, by my favorite author Aldous Huxley, tells the story of a culture that tests every innovation to understand its impact on society before it's rolled out. The book highlights the dangers of materialism, consumerism, and individualism, and suggests that a more compassionate and spiritually rich way of life—while embracing new technologies—is possible.

The positive force of innovation must be balanced with ethical considerations and the well-being of individuals, so that the innovations that win are aligned with shared human values.

I don't think we're quite there yet, but I trust that people can come together to digest and assimilate new technologies and create a meaningful cultural response. People are talking about AI now, with some saying it's nonsense because all the answers are wrong and others absolutely afraid of the machines taking over. What I'm seeing today is a clash of cultures between a freewheeling mindset where anything goes and an establishment mindset that says we have laws, rules, and traditions that demand respect.

I believe we need a constant rediscovery and reaffirmation of value systems within groups, from the team and corporate level all the way up to society. To optimize new technological opportunities, people are called to listen to each other and find common ground.

If we can figure out how to facilitate deep conversations among gifted individuals, we can get some truly fantastic projects off the ground. We just need to bring people together to share their feelings about technologies and new challenges they want to solve collectively, so they can reconcile their differences and move forward in alignment.

Advanced technology and the availability of information levels the playing field, and as innovation cycles get shorter and shorter it will become increasingly difficult for companies to differentiate themselves. We're entering an accelerated world where there'll be a startup every minute, but most of them will be gone almost as quickly.

Many will try, but only a few solutions will capture people's attention and go viral. And when that happens, it doesn't matter if there are a thousand comparable solutions out there. The viral one will become a unicorn. But again, because innovation will be so fast, winning won't be unique and in an instant we'll be on to the next thing.

"Looking at the earth from afar you realize it is too small for conflict and just big enough for cooperation."
—*Yuri Gagarin*

CHAPTER 10

BUILDING A TECH VALUE NETWORK: THE ULTIMATE END GAME

As business leaders and IT executives seek to digitally transform their companies at a faster pace, they're finding that traditional value chains don't meet their requirements for ramping up resources, transitioning people off projects at the right time, or adding different skills along the software development journey.

In the digital era, companies need a more flexible and scalable model that includes hyperspecialized talent on demand. I hear from managers all the time that they can't retrain their legacy people fast enough, that their current teams are overwhelmed, and that they want people who use more modern tools and have different business experiences to help them rethink existing capabilities and build new ones.

Gaining access to fresh thinking and new ways of solving problems often requires multiple outsourcing partners—often in different locations around the world—that can be tapped to meet changing needs for everything from e-commerce and mobile app development to bleeding-edge ventures into augmented reality, nanotechnology, and artificial intelligence. Often the more strategic roles aren't needed on a full-time basis, and we're constantly getting requests for people with specific types of expertise who can be hired part-time or as consultants.

In this shifting IT environment, a more adaptive, distributed supplier ecosystem is becoming the new norm. It's the rise of what I call tech value networks, alliances of professional software development firms—and individuals—that are ready, willing, and able to not only help clients get complex projects off the ground but are also game to collaborate with indirect and direct competitors to do so.

Accelerance helped pioneer this business model more than 20 years ago, resulting in the world's largest database of certified software development outsourcing firms ready for quick deployment. By putting a world of certified partners and specializations at our clients' service, they can scale their teams quickly regardless of the skills required at any given time.

More companies are creating similar networks of their own, within their geographies and beyond, as an extension of their businesses. Because few companies have a full range of in-house capabilities anymore, proactively assembling proven resources to manage the increasing acceleration and specialization of software technologies just makes sense.

Tech value networks deliver breadth as well as depth, helping businesses secure the most appropriate expertise from multiple partners, tapping into expert knowledge and scaling activity up and down as required.

This is particularly helpful as IT leaders need to make decisions about using and integrating technologies, programming languages, platforms, and concepts that they may still be working to grasp strategically—such as new cloud technologies, AI, the Internet of Things (IoT), robotic process automation (RPA), DevOps, and more. The ability to identify capable, potential partners early on to fill gaps—even before they arise—makes these decisions much easier to make.

When you have a tech value network in place, your business automatically becomes more resilient and future proof. You can pull in a wider range of skill sets at any given time, making you much nimbler and more competitive in a fast-paced marketplace. This type of network gives you fast access—within days, not weeks or months—to skills that are highly sought after and at the level of expertise you need for your projects.

Tech value networks mark the evolution of IT supplier models from tight, self-managed structures to more fluid, hub-and-spoke frameworks that can cover all the technologies you need today and might need tomorrow.

As you've no doubt come to understand, these connections to skilled resources are transcending borders. Centers of excellence in specialized areas of software development continue to emerge in Latin America, Central and Eastern Europe, South and Southeast Asia, and elsewhere around the globe. At the time of this writing, Egypt is pretty much the only major player in Africa to offer quality software development capabilities, but it won't be long before other African countries join the party.

As credible new partners get established, new relationships and cross-pollinations will be necessary to integrate the different technologies required for complex projects. This will put an even greater value on the ability to manage multinational teams. Soon, the majority of managers will move beyond having some team members in the U.S. and other team members in Costa Rica, for example, to having a core team at home, another core team offshore or nearshore, and a variety of specialists scattered around the globe.

Innovative IT leaders like Yogish Suvarna, currently Chief Information & Technology Officer at MyEyeDr., told the *National CIO Review* that the networked approach will be the next big thing. "One of the biggest challenges that every technology leader faces is sourcing the right talent at the right time to meet the constantly changing needs of the business," he said. "My advice is to surround yourself with innovative companies and partners who can help you and your team with meeting business needs and bridge the gap in your ever-changing talent needs."

Tech Value Networks in Action

So, what does a tech value network look like in practice?

Let's say you're the Chief Digital Officer for a supplier in the automotive industry that uses Salesforce to manage thousands of relationships, and that you want to get even more value from the platform. As your creative juices get flowing, different ideas pop into your head:

- What if you used AI-driven decision making to improve the sales of aftermarket parts to consumers?
- What if you could make your buyer portal easier to use?
- What if more of your customers could understand how to educate their buyers about diagnosis and troubleshooting to increase sales?
- What if you could strengthen the privacy and security of your customer data?

To create a suite of valuable capabilities with Salesforce at the core, you'll need software developers and engineers skilled in development methodologies and languages like Apex, Visualforce, Javascript, Lightning, Force.com, Heroku, and others. Because the people who possess these skills are often expensive, hard to find, and only needed on occasion, using a variety of outsourcing partners to obtain them on demand is the most practical way to go.

With a tech value network in place, all you really need to do is contact your go-to partners and get to work, putting the pieces of the puzzle together faster than you could do on your own—and faster than your competition. Using this focused, outcome-centric business model, your global partners play pivotal roles by providing best-in-class development talent—

general and specialized—that can plug in where they fit best for as long as they're needed.

Experts who follow software industry trends are seeing this approach take hold. "If I'm going to move quickly, I can't just grow my technology stack when I need to. So I'm increasingly dependent on third parties," says Bobby Cameron, Vice President and Principal Analyst at Forrester Research in a 2020 report. "I'm going to have shorter contracts with fewer players because I'm contracting for a platform—not all of the individual elements—and that allows me to move around the ecosystem to pick up the players I need to fill in holes I have."

Many of our clients at Accelerance have pursued, or are eager to pursue, a multi-vendor approach for rapid access to a variety of software development capabilities. For example, a major fintech company asked us to help them broaden their base of resources beyond a single time zone and continent. This gave them a larger recruiting pool and a larger network of connections, and it allowed them to reduce the risk of having all their eggs in one basket.

After identifying, onboarding, and managing new work processes, they can now find people to fill specific niche technology roles and reduce the firm's geopolitical risk.

As these types of expansive relationships mature, we're seeing new working arrangements emerge. Like-minded companies with similar requirements are banding together to offer work to outsourcing partners, benefitting from a greater surety of supply, partner loyalty, and even better pricing.

And, at the same time, the community of vendors is becoming more willing to share ideas and expertise in a spirit of collaboration.

With the ability to tap into a network of cooperative experts, companies have a better chance of gaining information that could change requirements before a project even starts. In the case of an emerging technology project, for example, you may decide to test out a new language instead of using a proven programming language—or vice versa, for that matter. Or you might use a combination of the two, or bring other programming languages into the mix. Having a tech value network gives you more people to contact for advice so you can make better, more informed decisions.

Build Your Own Tech Value Network

Like other aspects of multinational management, finding the right partners to include in your tech value network requires a new, expansive, and more open mindset. The traditional model of issuing formal RFPs and working through rounds of negotiations to find the most attractive suppliers is essentially dead. Lower-quality service providers have become adept at responding to RFPs, but when you meet them in person they're often not what they purported to be.

What you really want to do is find organizations that share your vision for networked collaboration. Way back in the early 1990s, organizational researcher James F. Moore coined the phrase "business ecosystem" in a 1993 *Harvard Business Review* article called "Predators and Prey: A New Ecology of Competition." He described the term as "an economic community supported by a foundation of interacting organizations and individuals—the organisms of the business world."

He went on to say that stakeholders throughout the ecosystem (including suppliers, lead producers, competitors, and others) "coevolve their capabilities and roles, and tend to align themselves with the directions set by one or more central companies. Those companies holding leadership roles may change over time, but the function of ecosystem leader is valued by the community because it enables members to move toward shared visions to align their investments, and to find mutually supportive roles."

The software development industry has been moving toward the establishment of these types of relationship-based networks for some time, although frankly, it's been hit or miss until recently.

In a fascinating paper called "Supply Chains and Value Webs," published by Deloitte University Press in 2015, authors Eamonn Kelly and Kelly Marchese pretty much predicted the rise of tech value networks in their description of how business ecosystems had come of age. "As ecosystems become more central to business strategy, the core value of the profession will be less and less in getting the same things done ever more efficiently, and more and more in the strategic pursuit of creating new value, achieving breakthrough performance, sustaining growth, and—once again—changing the world."

It all comes back to the unstoppable force of innovation that drives the most successful companies. And because of this, I truly believe that if firms create their own tech value networks, they'll be more likely to become ecosystem leaders.

Establishing your own tech value network is a worthwhile but complex challenge that may never stop evolving. You'll need to implement and manage new ways of working and processes for integration across your web of functions and relationships, including:

- New purchasing arrangements that see evolving and flexible configurations of partners, based on the business requirements for access to resources and skills
- Greater cooperation between formal and informal networks of suppliers and their customers, including knowledge sharing for best practices and performance
- New types of partnerships, outcome-driven incentives, and risk-reward terms that support building trusted, mutually beneficial relationships

You'll get the most out of a multi-partner network that evolves from a well-thought-out strategy. And, as you gain more experience outsourcing projects and managing multinational teams, you'll get a better sense of the resources you really need to reduce risks and costs while delivering desired business outcomes in a fraction of the time.

Companies used to hire people internally to write code, do capacity planning, maintain equipment, ensure security, and manage network load balancing. We still need all these things today, but with all the cloud platforms, code frameworks, and pre-built components available, it's never been easier to get started building software.

Any developer with a credit card can stand up a virtual infrastructure, but that doesn't mean they have the skills or knowledge to make it work. And it's the same with your internal team: They may be experts on how things have been done and are currently done at your firm, but they may not have the experience, the bandwidth, or even the motivation to take advantage of the new capabilities out there.

So you may need to expand your horizons for the supplemental and new technical skills you need to design with the architectures, security models, languages, and frameworks that can sustain your business needs.

Tapping into a tech value network allows you to move fast and break things, learning, filling in gaps, and adjusting the details of your plan within your overall development strategy. For example, you may need expertise in selecting a toolkit or framework, or maybe someone with deep database expertise to help get you on the right path. Or you might need help making sure that your system is as secure as you think it is, or planning how a new program will work with the existing systems you have.

The Benefits of the Network Effect

The right combination of partnerships creates value that's greater than the sum of its parts. (You'll learn more about that in this chapter's Guest Expert Spotlight.) When you have a network that's configured around specific providers contributing best-in-class skills to your organization's application development chain, you create a collaborative environment that inspires new ideas, streamlines work practices, and fosters continuous improvement to deliver benefits such as:

- Game-changing technology innovation
- Improved product quality and performance
- Lower development costs and increased efficacy
- Fewer IT-related business disruption risks
- More sophisticated data and insights

Troy Hiltbrand, our Guest Expert Spotlight contributor from Chapter 6, is one of our clients who was looking at building something of a tech value network from the start. "Our goal was always to have three competency centers, one in South America, one in Asia, and one in Europe," he told me recently. "The concept of multi-sourcing is very interesting because the strongest partners in each region still want to remain separate."

To solve the problem, Troy works hard to isolate his products so he can take one to Latin America, one to Asia, and one to Eastern Europe. And then he relies on each partner to pull in other resources they're comfortable working with, including specialists as needed, wherever they reside. It puts the burden of extended multinational management on his partners, but Troy says he only works with companies that have "figured out all the nuances of pulling together those international teams."

It all comes down to the essential questions this book has attempted to answer. How do you manage effectively across a wide variety of resources from different cultures? Do you take that on yourself? Do you try to find a partner that's already doing it? How do you vet their ability to manage teams across countries, cultures, and time zones themselves?

It's not an easy problem to solve, but if you crack the code of strategic resource allocation and cross-cultural collaboration, you can supercharge your development efforts with the perfect balance of speed, efficiency, cost, and quality.

The Future of Software Development Outsourcing

The global IT outsourcing market is expected to reach $1 trillion before 2030. In 2021, outsourcing accounted for 13.6% of the total IT budget, on average, and about 60% of companies outsourced at least some of their application development processes. If you're not currently outsourcing a significant portion of your software development and perfecting the way you manage multinational teams, it's going to be harder to catch up in the future.

But if you start now, benefit from the lessons I had to learn the hard way, and take the wisdom of the 10 guest experts who so graciously contributed to this book to heart, I do believe you'll be amazed at the results.

When Sheryl Sandberg was COO of Facebook, she said "When a company's culture aligns with its purpose, it becomes an unstoppable force, inspiring employees and driving innovation." This quote resonated with me the first time I heard it and I continue to relay it to employees and clients every chance I get.

I like it so much because it sums up my passion for creating cross-cultural teams to produce software that changes the world and improves the user experience.

Business leaders who know how to create and manage collaborative, multinational teams across a trusted tech value network benefit from a wider range of perspectives, ideas, and problem-solving approaches, without sacrificing the internal knowledge base they've worked so hard to create and build upon.

Through effective multinational management, organizations can harness this rich diversity of talent, worldviews, and experience for sustained growth and competitive advantage. I personally wish you well on your multinational management journey, and please know that I'm here if you need any assistance.

GUEST EXPERT SPOTLIGHT

RON LICHTY

Author of the renowned book "Managing the Unmanageable," Ron Lichty is a highly sought-after software engineering leadership and product development consultant. He helps companies of all sizes—from startups to the Fortune 100—transform chaos to clarity and make their software development hum.

Inspire Your People to Do Marvelous Work

Use the mechanisms of meaningful collaboration to get the most out of your teams.

More business is being conducted by teams these days, and the power of teams can't be overstated. The problem is that many managers aren't good at optimizing teams for maximum effectiveness. And I'm not just singling out engineering managers, I'm talking about everyone from the CEO on down.

So how do you do it? How do you get your people—regardless of their location, employee status, experience level, and area of expertise—to work well together? I believe it comes down to three things: communication, trust, and respect.

Too often in management we think that we'll just tell everybody what we're doing one time and they'll just get it. It doesn't matter if your people are all together in an office or scattered around the world, you've got to repeat your vision many times to get people to buy into it.

All the salespeople I know have a number in their heads. They've got to say something seven times or 17 times or whatever it is, but they know they won't sell something unless they've said it that many times.

It's the same with teams. Inspiring people, helping them understand what they're doing, and explaining how their individual contributions make a difference are some of the most important things you can do to get the most out of your teams, and you have to do them on a daily basis.

Managers and leaders must connect the dots between the work that individuals are asked to do and the impact it has on their mission, their customers, and their world. From your team members' perspective, they want to know what they're doing, why they're doing it, and what their social experience is going to be like. If you can satisfy those three elements, then you're well on your way to successful team management.

While I know this is a book about managing people no matter where they're located, I'm a firm believer in keeping the members of your teams as close together as possible. Research by Larry Maccherone, an expert on Agile, DevOps, and DevSecOps, showed that while co-located teams aren't necessarily better than distributed teams, it made a big difference if members of distributed teams were all in the same time zone. While this isn't always practical, I don't want to take a team and spread it across too many time zones because you lose opportunities to communicate the farther away you are.

Team members have to be able to talk to each other, collaborate, and interact. One company I was working with in San Francisco chose to work with a team in Spain. They could have chosen a closer Spanish-speaking country, but they chose Spain. By the time I arrived, I saw a group of people in Spain and a group of people in San Francisco: They were not functioning as a team.

To solve the problem, we brought everyone over from Spain to San Francisco for two weeks. We did three days of Agile training together. We did hackathons with small groups of people from both countries. We took a rural retreat. We shared lunches and dinners. And we created bonds that helped preserve team cohesiveness long after the people from Spain went back home.

What we knew we were doing during those two weeks was communicating the vision and aligning every team member around it. What we didn't exactly know we were doing was building a foundation of trust and respect, which is critical for high-performance teams.

You might have heard about Google's Project Aristotle. Google, just like the rest of us, has high-performance teams, low-performance teams, and teams that are in between. Unlike the rest of us, Google has a ton of money and they spent years trying to crack the code of what makes teams great.

Going in, the researchers thought they'd find some correlation between team success and team makeup, but the conclusion of Project Aristotle was that it doesn't really matter who's on a team at all. What matters most is how team members treat each other. With the right group norms—the cultural behaviors and unwritten rules that define social interactions—teams can become unstoppable, even if they're not filled with superstars. What I found most interesting about group norms is that they define how an individual acts on a team, even if it's not how that person operates elsewhere. In other words, group norms override individual proclivities.

The Project Aristotle researchers found that something called "psychological safety" has more to do with a team's performance than anything else. With group norms that build trust and respect, people are willing to take risks, make mistakes, admit vulnerabilities, and, most importantly, be themselves. When people are given the chance to express themselves freely, we have so much more to learn from them and they have so much more to give.

One of the key markers of teams with high levels of psychological safety is equality in conversational turn-taking. What this means is that members of the best-performing teams all talk about the same amount. Discussions are often freewheeling and spirited, but no one feels left out. Everyone feels heard and understood.

The other thing that distinguishes the best teams is a high degree of average social sensitivity, or the ability to use cues like tone of voice, body language, and facial expressions to understand how others are feeling. People on the high-performing teams at Google were found to do better at an exercise called the Reading the Mind in the Eyes Test, where you look at pictures of people's eyes and try to guess what they're feeling.

With these two things in place—conversational turn-taking and a high average social sensitivity—teams become supportive, energizing, and effective. Egos are left at the door, and domineering jerks need not apply. These teams may seem chaotic and disorganized to the outside observer, but they work. Stop for a moment and think about the teams you've been on and the ones you'd love to be on again. Chances are, your best experiences were on teams where the group norms created a whole that was greater than the sum of its parts.

I encourage you to take this information to heart and do whatever you can to build psychological safety on any team you ever get to manage. You may have to get creative, but it's worth it.

When I was working on a project with PSL in Colombia, they set up a product owner and a scrum master onsite in Medellin. The CEO and product management team were in Edmonton—the vision was in Edmonton—but it couldn't stay there if we were going to be successful. So the product owner in Medellin and the product manager in Edmonton got on the phone multiple times a day so they could get in sync with each other, answer questions, and keep things moving. With only an hour time difference, it was easy for them to stay in continuous contact.

According to international keynote speaker and bestselling author David Burkus, there are four things you can do as a manager to promote psychological safety:

1. Teach people to speak up and fight for their ideas, especially if the ideas are unique, because they might get chosen or create a vital discussion that leads to something else. This can be difficult for some people, for personal or cultural reasons, so you may have to give some team members more assistance in this area.

2. Celebrate failures as opportunities for learning. What I love about the Agile development process is that you get a chance to improve things at the end of every sprint. What one experiment could we try in the coming sprint that would make this different? If it doesn't work it doesn't work, and then we'll try something else.

3. Encourage dissent. If team leaders aren't okay with being wrong or vulnerable, no one else will be.

4. Model and build civility.

With skilled people scattered around the globe, you'll no doubt find yourself in a situation where you're managing multinational teams. Keep in mind that the best way to be successful is to inspire every team member with your vision, and then get every team member to inspire each other.

EPILOGUE

After all this, I'm going to go out on a limb and tell you that outsourcing is an outdated concept.

If you look at the world today, there's no such thing as outsourcing anymore because there's no other realistic way to do business in our global economy. In a world where talented people can live anywhere, and where centers of innovation can spring up anywhere, you have more options than ever before to go where the action is.

I sincerely hope you've come to realize that people are first and locations are secondary when it comes to forming teams. What pulls it all together is the art and science of multinational management—what I call Synergea—and if you can get that core competency nailed down I can pretty much guarantee you'll have job security for the rest of your career.

If it wasn't for search engines and the need to get high up in the Google rankings, I'd never use the word outsourcing to tell people about Accelerance again. But old habits die hard, and that's the term people seem to be searching for when they're looking for a company like ours.

So whether I like it or not, a curiosity about outsourcing is what brings people into the conversation with us. And we play along, knowing that eventually we'll have to tell the people who become our clients that what we're really going to do together is help them learn a whole new paradigm. When they're ready to hear it, we tell them that they're about to embark on an adventure that will enrich their businesses in dramatic ways.

Multinational management is bigger than outsourcing. It's about building trust and respect—psychological safety—on a global scale. It's about finding the best talent in unlikely places. And it's about opening yourself and others to personal and professional experiences that can be absolutely exhilarating.

You owe it to your current teams to gain a better understanding of—and appreciation for—different perspectives and different ways of working. Give them an inspiring team experience they'll remember for the rest of their lives, as they look back with pride on what they helped you accomplish when you pulled the rest of the world in close.

Photo Credit: Silvia Hilliard

ABOUT THE AUTHOR

Andy Hilliard has been advocating for globally collaborative software development teams since he started working at Cognizant in the 1990s. Since joining Accelerance, which he now serves as CEO, he's been responsible for connecting thousands of clients with quality nearshore and offshore development partners.

Feeding his passion for cultural appreciation and global business, Andy has visited more than 60 countries. Currently on his bucket list are South Africa, Portugal, and Pakistan.

Andy holds an MBA in International Business, Finance and Marketing from the Kellogg School of Management at Northwestern University. He lives in Kenwood, California and enjoys the magnificent wine country with his wife Silvia.

Email Andy at andy@accelerance.com.

ABOUT ACCELERANCE

Recognized as the Global Software Outsourcing Authority, Accelerance helps companies establish and scale high-performing, globally distributed software engineering and product development teams.

Using a proprietary and strategic client-partner matching system, we connect clients with external teams from our Certified Network of the top 1% of software outsourcing partners worldwide. Our Advisory Services further empower clients to organize, manage, and leverage these global software and product development partnerships efficiently toward valuable outcomes.

With a rich legacy spanning more than two decades, Accelerance stands unrivaled in nurturing globally distributed software and product development functions. Our unmatched authority in this ecosystem stems from a trust that has been earned and proven with businesses of all sizes in a wide variety of industries.

To learn more, visit accelerance.com.

Made in United States
Cleveland, OH
04 November 2026

47644437R00133